C000155231

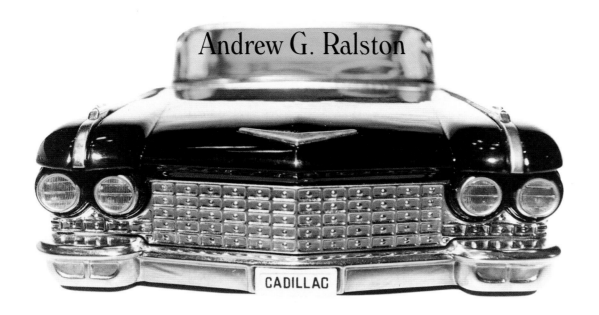

Andrew G. Ralston

Toy Cars
of
Japan and Hong Kong

Schiffer Publishing Ltd

4880 Lower Valley Road, Atglen, PA 19310 USA

DEDICATION

To Bruce Sterling, who probably knows more about Japanese toys than anyone else, and who encouraged me to write this book.

Copyright © 2001 by Andrew G. Ralston
Library of Congress Card Number: 00-104812

All rights reserved. No part of this work may be reproduced or used in any form or by any means—graphic, electronic, or mechanical, including photocopying or information storage and retrieval systems—without written permission from the copyright holder.
"Schiffer," "Schiffer Publishing Ltd. & Design," and the "Design of pen and ink well" are registered trademarks of Schiffer Publishing Ltd.

Designed by Bonnie M. Hensley
Type set in Windsor BT/Zurich BT

ISBN: 0-7643-1196-4
Printed in China
1 2 3 4

Published by Schiffer Publishing Ltd.
4880 Lower Valley Road
Atglen, PA 19310
Phone: (610) 593-1777; Fax: (610) 593-2002
E-mail: Schifferbk@aol.com
Please visit our web site catalog at **www.schifferbooks.com**

In Europe, Schiffer books are distributed by Bushwood Books
6 Marksbury Avenue Kew Gardens
Surrey TW9 4JF England
Phone: 44 (0) 20-8392-8585; Fax: 44 (0) 20-8392-9876
E-mail: Bushwd@aol.com
Free postage in the UK. Europe: air mail at cost.

This book may be purchased from the publisher.
Include $3.95 for shipping. Please try your bookstore first.
We are always looking for people to write books on new and related subjects.
If you have an idea for a book please contact us at the above address.
You may write for a free catalog.

CONTENTS

PREFACE

"Collectors," says the distinguished art historian Sir Kenneth Clark, "are basically of two kinds; those who aim at completing a series, and those who long to possess things that have bewitched them. The former, of whom stamp and coin collectors are the obvious examples, enjoy the pleasures of a limited aim, and its comforting certainties. The latter may suffer ups and downs, changes of heart and deceptions, but they have several great advantages. They never know when some new love will inflame them; they learn a great deal more about themselves from their possessions; and in the end they are surrounded by old friends, with long love stories which they must try hard not to tell to their friends."[1]

That definition is just as true of toy collectors as it is of those whose interest is in antiques, porcelain or fine art. If you belong to Clark's first category, the "series" collector, you may be disappointed to find that this book makes no attempt to provide an exhaustive list of every single toy made in Japan and Hong Kong, or every colour variation. Not only would that be an absurdly ambitious task anyway, but it would entail the cataloguing of many mundane items which are of little interest to anyone but the most fanatical collector who sets his heart on owning absolutely every replica ever made of a particular car no matter how poor a representation it might be.

On the other hand, if you are the kind of collector who "longs to possess things that have bewitched them", you will find much to aspire to as you go through the pages that follow. This volume is deliberately selective, focusing on the rarest and the best automotive toys to come out of Japan and Hong Kong between 1950 and 1970.

The first chapter traces the development of the Japanese toy industry from the time of the post-war American occupation until the early 1970s; the next two chapters illustrate some of the finest tinplate toys from this era, sold under names such as Asahi, Alps, Marusan, Ichiko, Yonezawa and Linemar.

Chapter Four discusses how some of the toy companies who previously used tinplate, plus other newcomers, started making 1/43 diecasts in the style of brands such as Dinky Toys and Corgi Toys. Major names here are Marusan, Model Pet and Cherryca Phenix.

In Chapters Five and Six the focus changes to Hong Kong, which gradually overtook Japan as a centre of toy production, with plastic replacing tin and diecast metal as the main raw material. It is only in the last few years that collectors have started to appreciate that 'made in Hong Kong' does not necessarily mean that a toy is of poor quality. This section of the book will reveal the existence of many excellent models that were until recently overlooked by collectors.

Often the background to toy production is as fascinating as the products themselves, and in each section of the book there will be an examination of the companies, the personalities and the manufacturing and distribution systems behind them.

ACKNOWLEDGEMENTS

Most of the company names and trademarks referred to in this book have long since disappeared, although some, such as Bandai, are still active in the toy business. These companies did not authorize this book or furnish or approve any of the information contained therein. Every effort has been made to trace the owners of trademarks and publications referred to in the book but this has not been possible in every case. The author and publishers will be pleased to include acknowledgement of such material in any future edition. This book is based entirely on the author's own research, but it would not have been possible without the help of numerous people:

Akiko Chihara, a former pupil of Hutchesons' Grammar School, Glasgow, devoted some of her scarce leisure hours to translating pages from a Japanese book on model cars for which no English translation is available in print.

Tin toy collector Mark Feigenson of New York provided copies of pages from an early Bandai toy catalogue which have been reproduced here.

Bart McNeil allowed an extract from his web page, *Tinplate Lithography on Jeep Toys,* to be reproduced on page 9.

Ms Janice McFarlane, Head of Reference Services at the National Library of Scotland, Edinburgh, kindly granted permission, on behalf of the Trustees of the National Library of Scotland, for the reproduction of the illustration of a Japanese toy factory on page 10.

Paul Jones, Deputy Editor of the British toy trade journal *Toy Trader*, gave approval for material to be reproduced from the earlier publication *Games and Toys*.

Hideyuki Kodama of Sega Toys Ltd, Tokyo, Japan went to enormous trouble to unearth scarce Yonezawa toy catalogues from his company's archives, and some of these are reproduced in this book.

Some of the information on Japanese tinplate cars first appeared in articles published in the British collecting journal *Model Collector* and the Editor, David Jinks, kindly allowed excerpts to be used here.

Professional photographer Steven Gibson of Glasgow took an interest in the whole project and the pictures of the models in part three of this book are typical of the high standard of his work.

Warren Cornelius, of London distributors W. H. Cornelius Ltd., explained how the toy distribution trade operated in the 1960s, and put the author in touch with Don Stephen, formerly Sales and Marketing Director of the British toy importers F. Levy and Company of London. Mr Stephen willingly shared his reminiscences of his involvement with the Hong Kong toy industry, bringing to light many fascinating pieces of information which have not appeared in print before.

Doug Kelly of Ashton, Maryland, USA generously supplied photographs of many unusual Japanese models, patiently responded to endless e-mail enquiries, and read sections of the book in manuscript. Doug is the author of the well-known *Die Cast Price Guide* (Antique Trader Books, Iowa, 1997) and the checklist of Japanese die cast cars on pages 154-155 is based on material from this book.

Alex Cameron of Stirlingshire, Scotland is the owner of one of the largest and most varied collections of model cars in Scotland, if not the whole of the United Kingdom, and can justifiably claim to be one of the very few collectors who recognised the appeal of Hong Kong plastic models long before anyone else started to look for them. Alex spent many hours digging out models from his collection for photographing—and just as many hours putting them back on his display shelves.

One of the world's finest collections of Japanese tinplate and diecast toys is owned by Bruce Sterling of New York, who not only allowed his models to appear in chapters Two, Three, and Four of this book, but cheerfully undertook the arduous task of photographing them himself. Few collectors have pursued "the things that have bewitched them" with as much determination and success. Quite literally, this book could never have been written without him.

And finally . . . a special thanks to my wife Hazel and daughter Miranda who—although they would never admit it—are actually quite interested in the toy collecting hobby.

Andrew G. Ralston
Glasgow, Scotland
June 2000

[1] Kenneth Clark, *Another Part of the Wood* (London, 1974), p. 193. Quoted by kind permission of the publishers, John Murray Ltd.

A NOTE ON VALUATIONS

The all-important question "what's it worth?" is not an easy one to answer. All that is possible here is to give a rough idea of a likely price range, compiled on the basis of personal experience, other published price guides, discussions with collectors and observation of prices at which items have recently been offered or sold. It can be stated with some degree of certainty that a model has been sold at some point for the price given here—but that does not mean that the next example of that model to reach the market will sell for the same price.

Geography is a factor that can affect the value of a Japanese toy. Some items are more sought after in one country than another. For instance, Model Pet and Micro Pet diecast Japanese cars are in great demand in Japan but do not have the same appeal in the USA. Similarly, Cherryca Phenix European cars are likely to achieve the best prices in France and Germany.

In the case of the diecast and plastic models discussed in Chapter Four and Six some sort of generally agreed "going rate" could be said to exist, and suggested prices are quoted after each picture caption. However, a different approach is taken with the larger tinplate cars pictured in Chapters Two and Three. It must be remembered that in some cases there may quite literally be no more than one or two mint and boxed examples of these in existence. These are the items that set new records whenever they appear at auction and for this reason, broad price bands are given, rather than precise figures.

There is always going to be one determined collector who will be prepared to pay whatever it takes to secure the item. Just occasionally, though, a very rare item can slip through the net and sell at a bargain price simply because the model was too obscure for the seller to realise its true worth.

Throughout the book the suggested prices refer only to examples in mint condition with their original boxes. As with other collectible toys, unboxed or non-mint items will be worth significantly less.

Price Categories

These codes are estimated price ranges that apply to Japanese tinplate toys pictured in chapters Two and Three:

1	$50–$100
2	$100–$150
3	$150–$250
4	$250–$300
5	$300–$500
6	$500–$750
7	$750–$1000
8	$1000–$1500
9	$1500–$2000
10	$2000–$3000
11	$3000+
12	$5000+
13	Over $10000

CHAPTER ONE

The Japanese Toy Industry, 1945–1970

Tinplate Jeeps began to emerge from Japan during the post-war American Occupation and were still being produced in the 1970s. This blue and red one is more colourful than most. *Courtesy of the Alex J. Cameron Collection.* $30

"A riddle wrapped inside a mystery inside an enigma." The words are those of Winston Churchill; though the subject was not toys, the description could aptly be applied to the Japanese toy industry. Certainly, there are a number of books available on this topic, such as those by Teruhisa Kitahara of the Yokohama Tin Toy Museum, and *Collecting the Tin Toy Car, 1950-1970*, published fifteen years ago by Dale Kelley. Kelley is the noted American collector and publisher of *Antique Toy World* magazine, which introduced many people—including the present author—to the magnificent variety of tinplate model cars made in Japan. These books, however, rely on their visual impact and do not attempt to provide historical or background information. In his introduction, Kelley expresses the hope that "in the years to come, as the hobby of collecting Japanese toys gains in popularity, more research will likely follow by toy collectors around the world"[1],

leading to new information on the structure of the Japanese toy industry. In the intervening decade and a half, however, little in the way of background about the companies that made these toys has been published, and the histories of the manufacturers remain shrouded in mystery.

Part of the reason lies in the fact that the structure of the toy industry in post-war Japan was very different from that of Europe or America. Imagine the economic state of Japan in 1945. The country had been defeated in war; cities lay in ruins; the disbanding of the military forces and the cessation of wartime production left an estimated ten million people out of work. Morale was at rock bottom and the country was in the hands of an occupying power, the United States.

And yet, some of these apparently negative factors worked in favour of the regeneration of the Japanese economy. There was an abundance of factory premises and skilled workers previously employed in military production whose skills were soon adapted to the manufacture of goods like sewing machines and cameras. During the war, much use was made of subcontracting of components, so that small firms developed specialised skills and learned to liaise with larger companies. Most important of all was the policy of the American occupiers. At first the aim was to restructure Japanese society in a more democratic way with economic recovery being seen as the responsibility of the Japanese themselves. From 1947 onwards, however, the Americans actively began to encourage Japan's economic strength so that the country might become a "bulwark against Communism" as the Cold War deepened.

These general factors have a great deal of relevance to the toy industry in particular. They explain, for instance, why the earliest toys to be made in Japan after the war tended to be American Army Jeeps, as these would be much in evidence at a time when there would be few other vehicles on the roads. Similarly, a plentiful labour force was at hand, which made the time-consuming process of printing colours onto tinplate sheets (a process known as lithography) an economically viable one. According to an interesting article on the Japanese toy industry which appeared in 1958 in an obscure British trade journal called *Toy and Game Manufacture*, it was the practice for some toy companies to contract out in rural areas where basic rates were below the national wage structure. The article claimed that the finishing of the majority of toys was carried out by workers at home, inevitably leading to cut-throat piecework rates.[2] Others—perhaps the better-finished ones—were entirely assembled in the one factory, as seems to have been the case with one of the finest of all Japanese tin cars, the Cadillac by Marusan. A sequence of photographs

Tinplate Lithography: How It's Done

Lithography ('drawing on stone'): An old printing process based on chemical reactions between oil and water. Its origins date back to 1798.

Printing hundreds and thousands of items in more than one colour demands absolute uniformity of size, shape, thickness, and smoothness of the surface to be printed. In the case of tin lithography, the tin is treated exactly like paper. It must be cut to exact dimensions. Each colour demands that the paper or tin go through the press again (for that particular paper). Some tin litho toys went through the press many times. It was a lot of work, but we are talking about very low-cost post-war Japanese labour. That's why they could do such great work so much cheaper than American manufacturers.

It has been suggested that tin cans were recycled to create some of the marvelous tin litho toys, but it would be next to impossible to use recycled tin cans and still maintain the accurate colour registration found on lithographed tinplate toys.

There is an alternative theory . . . more than likely the company which printed and manufactured the tin cans was the same one which manufactured the toys. It would not be unlikely that in manufacturing tin cans there could be a lot of imperfect printing on sheet tin (discovered before the can shapes were stamped out). The manufacturer could therefore use the reverse side of these to make toys.

Adapted from Tinplate Lithography on Jeep Toys: How It's Done *by Bart McNeil. See also http://www.apple.queensu.ca/CJ3B/Toys/JapanTinLitho.html*

Even a simple plaything like this little car and caravan trailer could involve numerous different lithographic printing operations and a good deal of assembly by hand. *Courtesy of the Alex J. Cameron Collection.* $30

taken around 1955 has recently come to light which gives a fascinating glimpse of various stages of the assembly process. The car bodies were stamped using old-fashioned hand presses, several of which appear to have been crammed into one room. Women workers put the various components together, and were photographed having their lunch break, which must have been a very brief one as they are still sitting at a table covered with Cadillac body pressings! The caption informs us that these workers were mostly housewives working for extra money who were paid approximately four shillings and sixpence a day[3], and that they brought their own meal of rice with them to work. The toy Cadillacs were turned out at the rate of 250 per day and sold for about four dollars, though it is not clear whether that was the trade or retail price.

Such methods allowed toys to be churned out in huge quantities, a process further stimulated by bulk orders from American department store buyers and toy importers. A 1956 report on the American toy market states that department stores accounted for 27% of total toy sales. When one considers that total U.S. toy sales that year were $1,250 million dollars, it is clear that a bulk order from a department store buyer could be a very significant one indeed. As such, buyers and importers—such as Cragstan of New York—could specify the product they wanted, which helps to explain some of the difficulties collectors have in identifying the makers of some Japanese toys of this period. The names that appear on the packaging of these toys are not necessarily those of the actual maker, but the distributor. Occasionally, a toy may have both

Lunch break at the Marusan factory c. 1955. Female workers eat their meals of rice while seated at their work tables, surrounded by toy Cadillacs in the course of assembly. *Courtesy of the Trustees of the National Library of Scotland.*

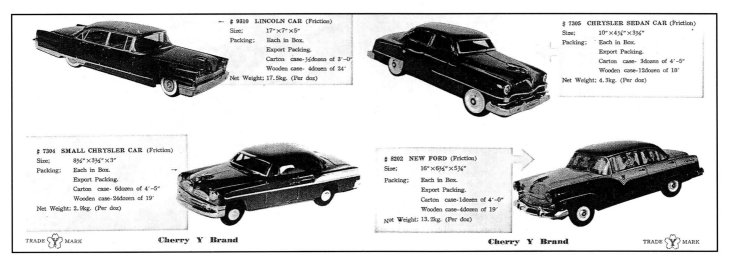

# 9310 LINCOLN CAR (Friction)			# 7305 CHRYSLER SEDAN CAR (Friction)
Size;	17"×7"×5"	Size;	10"×4¾"×3¾"
Packing;	Each in Box.	Packing;	Each in Box.
	Export Packing.		Export Packing.
	Carton case- ½dozen of 3'-0"		Carton case- 3dozen of 4'-5"
	Wooden case- 4dozen of 24'		Wooden case-12dozen of 18'
Net Weight; 17.5kg. (Per doz)		Net Weight; 4.3kg. (Per doz)	

# 7304 SMALL CHRYSLER CAR (Friction)			# 8202 NEW FORD (Friction)
Size;	8½"×3½"×3"	Size;	16"×6½"×5¼"
Packing;	Each in Box.	Packing;	Each in Box.
	Export Packing.		Export Packing.
	Carton case- 6dozen of 4'-5"		Carton case-1dozen of 4'-0"
	Wooden case-24dozen of 19'		Wooden case-4dozen of 19'
Net Weight; 2.9kg. (Per doz)		Net Weight; 13.2kg. (Per doz)	

TRADE 𝓎 MARK   **Cherry Y Brand**   **Cherry Y Brand**   TRADE 𝓎 MARK

Typical tinplate models of American cars illustrated in the 1964 Yonezawa trade catalogue. Note the ordering terms: the Chrysler Sedan, for instance, could be ordered in a carton containing three pieces, or in a wooden crate containing twelve dozen.

the Japanese maker's and the American distributor's name on it. This certainly happened with two of the biggest American toy distributors, Cragstan and Louis Marx. Many of Cragstan's toys were evidently supplied by Yonezawa, as both names can be found on some products, while Louis Marx actually had a Japanese subsidiary—Linemar—to make some of its tin and, later, diecast toys.

The growth in the export of Japanese toys to America received a further impetus after 1954 when the U.S. negotiated a tariff-cutting agreement on some 200 items to ease Japan's dollar shortage, covering goods such as jewelry, linens and toys. Some statistics relating to Japanese toy production have survived that give an indication of just how rapid this growth was. In 1961, for example, 24.5 million cases of toys were produced—an impressive enough figure in itself, but even more staggering when it is taken into account that the toys were packed one dozen to a case! 80% of this total output was exported, 60% of total output going to the United States, and $12 million of Japanese toys went to Europe. 43% of the total 1961 exports of $83 million were described as metallic toys—a large proportion of these presumably being tinplate cars of the type we are concerned with.[4]

Trouble in Toytown

All this might help to regenerate the Japanese economy, increase the profits of toy retailers, and bring delight to children, not to mention adult collectors today. But the growth of the toy industry in the East brought no pleasure to established toy manufacturers in Europe who began to complain about unfair competition. "The British Toy Manu-

An eight-inch tinplate "Lite-it-up" Ford by Ichiko. The battery-operated lights could be switched on or off by moving the lever on the side of the bodywork. These toys were primarily made for the American market. *Courtesy of the Alex J. Cameron Collection.* $100

facturing Industry cannot be other than concerned at the increasing flood of imports particularly of cheap and low quality toys . . .There can be little valid argument against the equity of competition from manufacturers whose conditions of production are comparable to those in this country, but neither in Japan nor in Hong Kong are working conditions such as would be tolerated by the Government."[5]

After simmering for some years, this problem came to a head in 1959. For half a century, the town of Brighton on the south coast of England has hosted an annual Toy Trade Fair. Such events offer opportunities for buyers to see new product lines and for business deals to be secured—hardly the stuff of newspaper headlines. But the 1959 Brighton Toy Fair was different. In that year, open hostility broke out between the British Toy Manufacturers' Association, led by their chairman Mr. Arthur Katz, managing director of Mettoy, and Japanese delegates to the fair. All members of the Association decided, most inhospitably, that they would refuse to show their products to the Japanese who, they claimed, would simply steal their ideas and copy them in their own factories. As one British toymaker put it at the time, "it's one thing to let your business out of the back door and quite another to put down the red carpet and sweep your business out of the front."[6]

That unedifying episode sums up what many people thought—and perhaps still think—about the toys made in the Far East. Lack of imagination in product choice; illegal copying of other manufacturers' lines; mass production in cheap quality materials—accusations such as these were repeatedly levelled against the Japanese toy industry at the time. Needless to say, the Japanese strongly rejected these criticisms. In April, the *Times* reported Mr Yoshihiro Kishi, president of a leading toy firm, as saying that what he saw in Brighton gave him the impression that "the British toy industry is at such a low level that we would not even begin to think of copying its products."[7] He even offered to arrange for delegates of the British toy trade to inspect Japanese toy factories.

When the Japanese went to the equivalent trade show in Germany, at Nurnberg, they did not receive any warmer a welcome. A Japanese newspaper carried a report by the interpreter for the Japanese delegation to Nurnberg, Professor Fujita, who said that a meeting between German and Japanese toy trade representatives had been held at which the Germans strongly condemned the Japanese for blatantly copying their products. Rather ominously, Professor Fujita writes that his delegation "had to admit that there were some unscrupulous Japanese manufacturers and they promised to root them out as soon as they got home."

For all the mutual mud-slinging, it is clear that by this time the Japanese toy industry was becoming more organized and westernized in its approach. A trade report from December 1962 states that 360 small manufacturers of metal toys were clustered in the Katsushika and Sumida districts of Tokyo, suggesting that the earlier methods of subcontracting assembly to workers at home might have been dying out. In 1960 Japanese toymakers started to co-operate with each other by ending price warfare amongst themselves and setting up a committee of makers of metal toys to decide a 'floor price' for new designs. Similarly, steps were taken to ensure that products complied with Japanese Industrial Standards. During the Occupation the initiative was taken by wholesale buyers from overseas, but in 1962 the manufacturers themselves organized the first Japanese International Toy Fair in the Tokyo Trade Centre. Japanese companies similarly began to exhibit their own products at

The Bandai toy factory as it was in the 1960s.

By the late 1960s battery-operated tin cars had largely replaced friction-driven ones, as this page from the 1968 Yonezawa catalogue shows.

European and American toy fairs: the Asahi Trading Company, for instance, collectively represented nine Japanese toy firms at the 1964 Nurnberg Toy Trade Fair.

By 1967 toy manufacture was becoming so efficient that a number of companies were prepared to take co-operation further still. *Toys International* magazine carried a report intriguingly entitled 'The Toy-Town on the Peanut Farm'. "Some sixty miles outside Tokyo," it read, "is Omochano-Machi, the Toy-Town. That is the name on the station, and it means exactly what it says. Omochano-Machi is a complex of small toy manufacturers located together in one area in an association which this year will have a total production of £2,500,000."[8] This 190-acre site, formerly a peanut farm, was taken over by 58 smaller toy manufacturers who decided to leave their overcrowded premises in Tokyo. By banding together to form their own Association of Exporting Toy Manufacturers, they were able to operate a central buying system, and by handling their own sales could avoid the commission of up to 50% previously expected by conventional wholesalers. One of the companies in the new complex was Tomy, established in 1953 and now a major manufacturer of computer software, video games and pre-school toys.

By the mid-1960s, then, it could be said that the Japanese toy industry had moved far beyond the ad hoc arrangements that grew up after the war and was now organized on more modern lines, with the American buyers and distributors being of less significance. Products were becoming more sophisticated, too: as early as 1962 it was reported that sales of friction and clockwork-powered toys were falling as those of battery-operated toys increased. Later on, Japanese progress in electronics would not only affect future toy designs but would lead to the development of new and technologically innovative industries at the expense of the older ones like toys, textiles and ceramics. At

A selection of Yonezawa products on the cover of the 1967 catalogue. These ranged from the traditional tin cars, robots, and mechanical animals to 1/43 scale diecast cars.

the same time, increasing prosperity created a much greater domestic demand for toys in Japan itself.

Although knowledge of the histories of individual Japanese companies is hard to come by in the West, these generalizations would hold good for most of them. Companies that did not adapt in this way simply did not survive. A look at the development of two of the best known—Yonezawa and Bandai—

Naoharu Yamashina, founder of Bandai Toys.

is instructive in this respect. Thanks to a recently discovered sequence of trade catalogues kindly supplied by Sega Enterprises, Ltd. (who bought over Yonezawa), it has been possible to trace the evolution of Yonezawa's product line in the decade from 1963 onwards. In 1964, for instance, virtually the whole of Yonezawa's inventory consisted of tin toys, cars being only one of many such lines: clockwork train sets on the Hornby pattern, numerous buses and fire engines, aircraft, large push-along railway engines and plush-covered mechanical toys—one being the 'Piggy Cook', a pig wearing a chef's hat who pours ingredients into his saucepan! Almost every one of these had some kind of clockwork or friction mechanism, although a few had hand-held battery remote controllers. Ten years

on, the Yonezawa catalogue contains numerous cars and trucks which are not dissimilar in appearance to the 1964 range, but battery-operated cable-link controls have now been superseded by the wireless radio-control method of operation, and a large proportion of the catalogue is now made up of 'Diapet' diecast cars with opening parts as fitted on Dinky or Corgi Toys. Nevertheless, this progress was not sufficient to ensure the survival of the company which was eventually taken over by the vast Sega corporation, best known today for their computer games. Sega Yonezawa Ltd of Haneda Ota-ku, Tokyo, is still listed as one of the many subsidiaries of Sega Enterprises.

The Bandai company, on the other hand, has had rather more success in adapting to changing

BATTERY OPERATED   ACTION TOYS   Bandai

KINGSIZE SERIES

NEW 4295 KINGSIZE FORD MUSTANG FASTBACK
Size: 13¾ inches long
½ dozen per chip
1 dozen per carton
24.0 lbs. per carton

NEW 4296 KINGSIZE CADILLAC CONVERTIBLE
Size: 13 inches long
½ dozen per chip
1 dozen per carton
24.0 lbs. per carton

4295   KINGSIZE FORD MUSTANG FASTBACK
∗ Bump and go action with motor sound. ∗ While it runs, green light lights up at rear window. ∗ When it stops automatically, door opens and figure "STOP" in red appears at rear window and blinks. Then door closes and starts again.
∗ Takes 2 UM-1(D-CELL) batteries.
4296   KINGSIZE CADILLAC CONVERTIBLE   ∗ Runs forward and reverse by shifting gears. ∗ Drop seats with steering wheel. ∗ Steering wheel operates front wheels. ∗ Horn honks by pushing steering wheel. ∗ Speed controllable by shifting levers. ∗ Headlights and engine are controlled at dashboard. ∗ Takes 2 UM-1(D-Cell)

A page from the 1969 Bandai trade catalogue. While the resemblance to earlier tin cars is clear, by the late sixties/early seventies an increasing use of plastic was evident. By this stage Bandai and other Japanese firms were subcontracting manufacture to other countries with developing economies such as Korea. The golden age of the tin toy was over.

times and tastes. Its founder, Naoharu Yamashina, originally worked in the textiles business but became aware of the opportunities in the toy industry during the years of the American occupation. From distributing toys he began to introduce original lines, the first being a beach ball with a bell inside called the 'Rhythm Ball' and by the mid-fifties was exporting to America the tinplate cars which are so sought after today by collectors. Thereafter, Bandai concentrated on the domestic market but had great worldwide success with action figures such as Power Rangers and then with Tamagotchi virtual pets. Yamashina died in 1997, saddened that his company, like Yonezawa, was about to link up with Sega—although that deal did not in fact come about. With a turnover of $1.6 billion in 1996, the Bandai corporation had come a long way from its humble beginnings.

From Japan to Hong Kong

The increasing sophistication of Japanese toys created a new opportunity for another developing economy to supply the market for cheap toys that had been the foundation of Japan's success fifteen years earlier. There is, in fact, an economic cycle that operates in the toy industry. The pattern seems to be as follows: a country undercuts its competitors as a result of the availability of cheap labour. Expertise in designing such toys may be lacking, leading to copying of already existing product lines. However, technical skill is quickly acquired and products become more sophisticated, resulting in better quality and increased price. At this point, someone else starts to copy these products, making them in another country where labour rates are cheaper, and the economic cycle starts again.

This pattern was evident even in nineteenth-century Germany, perhaps the first nation to have an established toy industry. Henry Mayhew, whose research into the lives of humble workers in the 1850s was published as *London Labour and London Poor*, recounts a conversation he had with "a large toy dealer in High Holborn". The dealer gave the following picture of the German toy industry in its early stages:

English toys are well made—such as rocking horses and large things; but in smaller things the English workmen can't pretend to vie with the Germans . . . Nuremburg, Frankfort and the vicinity of the Black Forest, are the principal places in Germany where these toys are made.

Women, children and poor people, with hardly any food to eat, make them and take them to merchants who export them . . .They starve in trying to outdo one another in cheapness, which injures them and is no benefit to the tradesman. . . The makers don't live, but starve, by it.[9]

Change the place names and that description could equally well apply to Japan in the 1930s and, even more so, in the period after World War II. Many of the great names of the German tin toy industry—Karl Bub, Arnold, Kellerman, etc.—struggled to re-establish themselves after the war but eventually disappeared as they could not compete with the Japanese.

Chapter Five of this book will explain how the same economic cycle was repeated when Hong Kong overtook Japan as the world's major producer of toys. The very same accusations—cheap quality, imitation of other people's products—were levelled against Hong Kong. While these were as true of the earliest Hong Kong toys as they had been of the earliest Japanese ones, quality soon improved and more imaginative product designs emerged. Although it is outside the scope of this book, it's worth pointing out that in the 1980s and '90s, Hong Kong in turn has been superseded by China as the world's main toy supplier. A similar pattern of development took place in China's Guangdong province as occurred in Japan in the fifties and Hong Kong in the sixties. In the toy industry, as in most other aspects of life, it seems, history repeats itself.

References

[1]Kelley, Dale. *Collecting the Tin Toy Car, 1950–1970,* New Cavendish Books, London, 1984, p. 8
[2]Article on 'The Japanese Toy Industry', in *Toy and Game Manufacture*, March 1958, pp. 15–18.
[3]Four shillings and sixpence in pre-decimal British currency would be 22.5 pence or 33.75 cents today.
[4]*Games and Toys*, December 1962, p. 42
[5]*Toys and Fancy Goods*, April 1962, p.25
[6]Reported in *The Times*, February 20, 1959
[7]*The Times*, April 7, 1959
[8]*Toys International*, September/October 1967, pp. 22–23
[9]Mayhew, Henry. *The Morning Chronicle Survey of Labour and the Poor: the Metropolitan Districts,* Volume 3, Caliban Books, Horsham, Sussex, 1981

CHAPTER TWO

Tinplate American Cars

This yellow cab is typical of most people's idea of a Japanese tin toy: cheap and cheerful, it has a naive charm which, together with its delightful box art, gives it an obvious and immediate appeal to the toy collector. Huge quantities of such toys were mass-produced in Japan from the time of the American Occupation onwards, and most of them went straight to the United States.

Low labour rates made quality possible as well as quantity. The purpose of this chapter is not to attempt to cover the whole spectrum of Japanese tin toy production, but to concentrate exclusively on the very finest pieces. In this case, the best are invariably the biggest, most being at least eight inches in length with some extending to as much as sixteen or seventeen inches. It is not as easy to replicate the complex curves of a motor vehicle in a medium like flat tinplate, as in injection-moulded diecast metal. It is the larger tin toys, often made in two or more separate sections, that succeed in capturing the true proportions of the original. Quite simply, it is this realism that differentiates the best tin toys from all the others. Every model pictured in this chapter is a more or less accurate likeness of a particular prototype.

Don't expect to find toys like these at the average collectors' fair. They are so scarce that those which do come up for sale generally surface at auctions where they frequently achieve record prices. Some of those pictured are thought to be among a mere handful of examples known to exist in pristine, boxed condition. Almost all of them come from the collection of Bruce Sterling of New York, who has spent a lifetime seeking out the very best examples of tinplate toys.

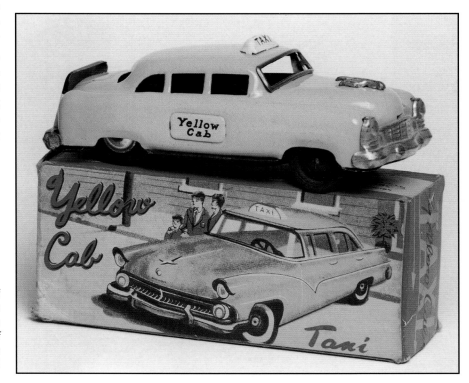

This five-inch taxi, marked ASC, is typical of many simple Japanese tinplate cars. The toy inside bears little resemblance to the 1955 Ford pictured on the box. *Courtesy of the Alex J. Cameron Collection.* Price Category: 1

1950–53 Cadillacs

Since Cadillac is the most prestigious name in the American motor industry, it is not surprising that the Japanese chose to model cars of that marque. Most tin toy collectors would agree that the best of them all was the Marusan.

Attention to detail on Japanese tin toys is always impressive, yet the overall proportions often leave something to be desired: the wheelbase can be too narrow, the roof too high, and so on. But the shape of Marusan's Cadillac perfectly captures the massive dignity of the original. They got the details right,

too, with correctly proportioned window surrounds, boot and bonnet motifs, number plates and even the Cadillac badges and script being represented by separate tin components. Identification is not a problem with this model, as both the box and the base carry the name "San" or "Marusan". The shape of the model is based on body styling used by Cadillac between 1950–1953 which replaced the former split windshield with a one-piece screen, but retained the tail fins of Harley Earl's 1948 design. The performance of the car's V8 331 cubic inch engine became legendary: it was even claimed that up to 90 mph the heavy Cadillac was faster than a Jaguar.

Few other Japanese tin toys were as well-proportioned or as skilfully put together as the magnificent Cadillac by Marusan. *Courtesy of the Bruce Sterling Collection.* Price Category: 8

Close-up of the front of the Marusan Cadillac. *Courtesy of the Bruce Sterling Collection.*

Rear view of the Marusan Cadillac, showing details such as the Cadillac crest and license plate. *Courtesy of the Bruce Sterling Collection.*

This sober, dignified gray shade suits the Marusan Cadillac well. *Courtesy of the Bruce Sterling Collection.* Price Category: 8.

If the real car could out-accelerate a Jaguar, the tinplate version was a little slower. Those fitted with a friction mechanism carried a box label warning the purchaser that the friction drive only operated on one rear wheel, while electrically-powered cars carried their batteries in a compartment concealed in the base, causing such a strain on the motor that the vehicle could barely crawl along the floor. These toys didn't only have electric motors; the batteries allowed the lights to work too.

The electric Cadillac is known to exist in all-over gold, or in pale yellow with a dark green roof.

One unusual variation had a more complex mechanism with an extra control on the base allowing the car to travel in various pre-set directions such as forwards, backwards, or a figure of eight. This version has been seen in yellow with an orange roof.

All Marusan Cadillacs are rare, of course, but the friction-driven ones are, comparatively-speaking, more easily obtainable than the electric ones. At least four colours have been recorded: black, white, gray and red. There was also a black and white Police livery. Gray colour schemes can often end up looking rather somber, but the blue-gray shade chosen by Marusan gives the car a dignified appearance and sets off the gold detailing of the front and rear "V" motif very effectively.

There's an interesting sequel to the history of the Marusan Cadillac. As we saw earlier, European—particularly German—toy manufacturers loudly complained that their designs were blatantly copied by the Japanese. Copying in the other direction wasn't so common, but with the Cadillac the Germans got their own back, as a very similar car appeared from the long-established firm of Gama.

A comparison of the Marusan (front) and Gama (back) Cadillacs. Note the different treatment of the windscreen frame. *Courtesy of the Bruce Sterling Collection.*

The batteries for the Gama model were contained in a separate control box. *Courtesy of the Bruce Sterling Collection.* Price Category: 6.

We've already seen how the American presence in Occupied Japan influenced the tin toys made there. But the Americans also had a high profile in post-war Europe. As Gerhard Walter points out in *Tin Dream Machines*, his definitive history of the German tin toy industry, many American army officers brought their own cars over to Germany, where their spell of duty might last for several years. It is easy to imagine the impact that such huge, ostentatious machines would have had in the bomb-ravaged streets of Berlin, and that's probably what led Gama to make their most impressive tin toy ever.

The Gama Cadillac looks so like the Marusan that it is either a direct copy or even, perhaps, made from the same moulds. But a closer examination of the two models shows that things are a little more complicated than that. The Gama has a curved wrap-around screen which was characteristic of the 1954 Cadillac—a fact confirmed by the box illustration. The grille is different, too. What Gama did was simply to update the grille and superstructure and fit these parts onto the original early fifties body shape, thereby creating a hybrid that never really existed at all! Like the Marusan, the model was powered by friction or electric motor, in this case operated by a hand-held battery controller.

There was yet another footnote to the history of the Cadillac: Gama later sold the tooling to Joustra of Strasbourg in France, who continued to produce it for a few more years. Joustra added their own name on the rear parcel shelf—but left the Gama badging on the front and rear!

About a year after they started making the sedan, Gama took further liberties with the Cadillac and introduced a convertible, fitted with a radio aerial and a driver made of the "composition" material commonly used at the time for toy soldiers. The convertible was simply the same toy without a roof—resulting in a four-door convertible which never existed either.

This mistake had already been made by another Japanese manufacturer, Nomura, whose toys can be identified by the "TN" trademark. Their model, which is shown here in pale gray, is altogether a cruder likeness than either the Marusan or the Gama. The tin is not nearly as cleanly moulded and the arrangement of the rear light cluster is not accurate. But one is not always looking for total accuracy from a tin toy, of course, and the TN still has many appealing features, not least the beautifully lithographed interior and the ingenious dashboard controls. Forward and reverse movements are controlled by the "gear lever" on the steering column, and the switch on the other side of the dash turns the lights on. The front bench seat tips forward to allow access to the battery storage compartment.

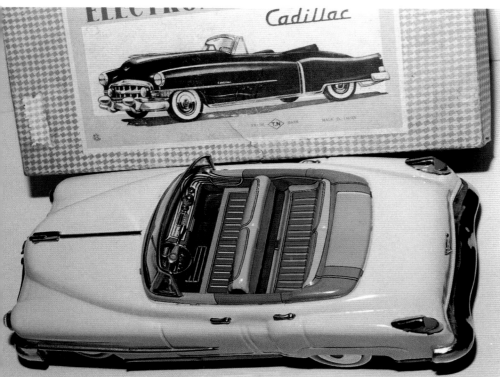

The Cadillac convertible by TN has four doors, unlike the real car, which only had two. *Courtesy of the Bruce Sterling Collection.* Price Category: 6.

Rear view of TN's Cadillac convertible.
Courtesy of the Bruce Sterling Collection.

A further Cadillac convertible was made in Japan around the same time as the TN version, this time by Alps. Both cars are based on the 1952 Series 62 convertible, but the Alps version is slightly smaller in length (about eleven inches) and has bodywork that reflects the real car in having only two doors.

Unlike many tin toys, the friction drive mechanism on the Alps Cadillac does not protrude into the seating area, so that the interior details on this model are its most remarkable feature. Even the grab handles on the back of the seats are there.

Many colour variations of the Alps can be found, among them red, maroon, gray, metallic green, light blue and, most frequently, black.

Cadillacs of the Early Sixties

Cadillacs continued to be a popular choice for tin toys in the early sixties. Those shown here are by no means the only ones made, but they're certainly a good cross-section of the most desirable tin toys of Cadillac's "tail fin" period.

Bandai made eleven-inch versions of both the 1959 and 1960 cars, the main difference between them being the size of the tail fins. Both cars also came as non-prototypical convertibles, and an example of the 1960 model is shown here. The white 1960 sedan is slightly smaller, about 9.5 inches long, and is all the more desirable for being in a box carrying the brand name "S & E," about which little is known. But it doesn't capture the long, low look of the original nearly as well as the black Yonezawa. Admittedly, the Yonezawa has the advantage of being almost twice the length of the S & E, a size which makes it easier to get the proportions right. Known to exist in both black and dark metallic red, this toy has separately attached cream-coloured side inserts and detailed lithographed wheel trims.

If the Yonezawa made the best 1960 Cadillac, SSS made the best '61. As the box states, this is based on a Fleetwood Seventy-Five and its large dimensions (17.5 inches in length) allow for extra features like an open-

This version of the Cadillac, by Alps, has the correct two-door arrangement. *Courtesy of the Bruce Sterling Collection.* Price Category: 9

Yonezawa's impressive eighteen-inch 1960 Cadillac is notably successful in capturing the massive lines of the original car. *Courtesy of the Bruce Sterling Collection.* Price Category: 9

The Cadillac looks equally good from the rear. *Courtesy of the Bruce Sterling Collection.*

Close-up of the grille of the Yonezawa model. *Courtesy of the Bruce Sterling Collection.*

Close-up of the rear of the Yonezawa. *Courtesy of the Bruce Sterling Collection.*

ing bonnet and trunk. This model is also known in black and a rather less appropriate two-tone green.

It has already been noted that the practice of making the coachwork of tin toy sedans in two halves—upper and lower—enabled convertibles to be produced with comparatively little modification, the downside being that these still retained the four-door arrangement of the sedans, something rarely found on real cars for structural reasons.

In the case of the '61 Cadillac, however, SSS didn't just chop off the roof but fitted several extra features that made the toy more fun for a child to play with. Top of the list was a remarkably clever "dual action" system allowing either friction or electric power to be selected. It worked like this. The "gear lever" on the steering column could be moved down to allow the car to be played with manually, on friction power. Moving the lever upwards en-gaged the electric option and a turn of the dashboard key—right for forwards or left for backwards—would light up the ignition warning lamp and set the engine fan rotating under the bonnet. No wonder the box describes the car as offering "magnificent play value"! Other novel touches included a "flock" interior and a "Cadillac" pouch for the ignition key.

Bandai's eleven-inch 1960 convertible is simply the sedan with the roof removed. *Courtesy of the Bruce Sterling Collection.* Price Category: 5

The 1961 Cadillac by SSS towers over the smaller 1960 model from S & E. *Courtesy of the Bruce Sterling Collection.* SSS, Price Category: 9; S & E, Price Category: 4.

1961 Cadillac Fleetwood by SSS. *Courtesy of the Bruce Sterling Collection.*

Like the earlier TN convertible, the SSS has four doors rather than two. *Courtesy of the Bruce Sterling Collection.* Price Category: 9

Close-up of the rotating cooling fan on the convertible version of the SSS Cadillac. *Courtesy of the Bruce Sterling Collection.*

Luggage compartment of the SSS Cadillac. *Courtesy of the Bruce Sterling Collection.*

Moving the gear shift on the SSS Cadillac engages either electric or friction power. *Courtesy of the Bruce Sterling Collection.*

A few years later, Bandai brought out a rather similar toy which makes an interesting comparison with the SSS model. At seventeen inches in length, the Bandai is of a comparable size. Described on the box simply as a "Golden Cadillac Convertible," it seems to be a 1963 model when viewed from the front—and a '61 when viewed from the back! As on the SSS version, there's a steering column lever and an ignition key, but this time the lever has forward, neutral, and reverse positions and the key works as an on/off switch. There's no electric fan but there are separate switches for front and rear lights, and

the horn operates as well. Both cars have an opening trunk, but in the Bandai's case this is a functional feature, as the luggage compartment is used to store the batteries. A difference is that the Bandai has two rather than four doors, and they actually open.

The last Cadillac shown is a 1963 or '64 hardtop from Ichiko. This, too, has an unusual gimmick: a "moving speed meter" on the dash with an arrow that moves along when the friction motor is revved up. There seems no limit to Japanese ingenuity!

The side doors open on Bandai's "Golden Cadillac." *Courtesy of the Alex J. Cameron Collection.* Price Category: 5

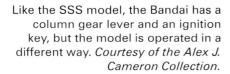

Like the SSS model, the Bandai has a column gear lever and an ignition key, but the model is operated in a different way. *Courtesy of the Alex J. Cameron Collection.*

The car illustrated on the box of the Bandai Cadillac is not quite the same as the model inside. *Courtesy of the Alex J. Cameron Collection.*

Ichiko's Cadillac hardtop features an ingenious working speedometer. *Courtesy of the Bruce Sterling Collection.* Price Category: 5

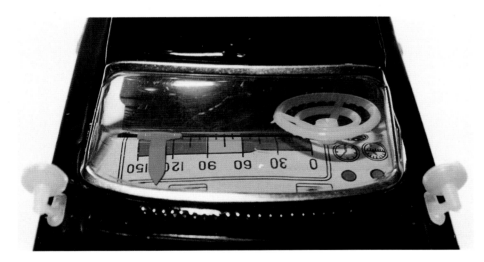

Close-up of the "speed meter" on the Ichiko. *Courtesy of the Bruce Sterling Collection.*

1950s Buicks

For many years Buick had an advertising slogan which read: "When Better Automobiles are Built, Buick will Build Them." But when Marusan made a model of a Buick, it wasn't one of *their* best automobiles. The box described it as "sister car of our famous Cadillac," but compared to that tinplate masterpiece the Buick was something of an anticlimax.

For one thing, it's much smaller—7.5 inches in length—and its overall proportions are far more squat and toylike. That's a pity, as the detailing is good, particularly the treatment of the front grille and the trademark Buick "portholes" along the front fenders. The model represents a Roadmaster from 1953—the year Buick celebrated its golden anniversary and the year that it introduced a new ohv V-8 engine.

The '53 Buick by Marusan is more "toy-like" than the same firm's Cadillac. The assembled model is less common that the constructional version. *Courtesy of the Bruce Sterling Collection.* Price Category: 6

More colour variations on the '53 Buick. *Courtesy of the Bruce Sterling Collection*

Sister car of our famous
"Cadillac" favoured by our young
friends. Smaller, but now appeared
with LIGHTS. A toy, but more than a toy.
Another hit item for this year produced by
MARUSAN

SCALE MODEL AUTO KIT
WITH OPERATION LIGHTS

此のビュイクは

These disassembled Buicks reveal the method of fitting the battery, which powered the electric lights. *Courtesy of the Bruce Sterling Collection.* Price Category: 5

Marusan also made this entirely different version of the Buick, fitted with a remote control mechanism. The front wheels are permanently angled and can be straightened by moving the lever on the control box to allow the car to change direction. *Courtesy of the Bruce Sterling Collection.* Price Category: 5.

Unusual for Japanese tin cars of this period, Marusan's Buick came in "kit" form, not totally disassembled, but with the body separate from the chassis. The reason was that the car had battery-operated electric lights as well as a friction motor, and the battery clipped into the inside of the chassis before the bodywork was fitted on top. This was the main selling feature of the toy, and the less exciting fully-built version with simple chrome headlights is actually harder to find. Black tends to be the most common colour for the Buick, with maroon being the rarest.

One of the many strange aspects of Japanese tin toys is that manufacturers might make very similar toys in different sizes. As well as the 7.5-inch Buick, Marusan made an 8.5-inch one, but it's not quite the same: the smaller car is a two-door with a non-prototypical split windshield and the larger one is a four-door sedan. This Buick is an early attempt at the remote-control type of toy, being powered by a hand-held battery box with a lever that operates the steering. Steering movements are very basic, as the front wheels are permanently set at an angle and the lever simply straightens them.

1958 Buicks

Five years can be a long time in terms of American car design, and the difference between 1953 and 1958 Buick styling is remarkable. Whether it was an improvement is another matter. In the opinion of the *Consumer Guide to Cars of the 50s*, 1958 produced "the ugliest Buicks in history." But an ugly car need not result in an ugly model, as the two versions by Bandai and Asahi illustrate.

The Bandai is from the small 8-inch series and is one of the relatively few tin toys that represents a four-door sedan rather than a two-door hardtop. (That same preference for two-doors persists in the diecast market to this day, as in the recent "Racing Champions" series, for instance. No doubt toy manufacturers feel that two-door hardtops are more "sporty" than four-door sedans). Even though the roof section looks like it should be fitted a little further forward, the Bandai is still a decent likeness. And the box, of course, is a work of art in itself. Bandai did this Buick as a convertible and a station wagon as well.

The ATC (Asahi) is both larger—14.5 inches—and rarer, with a box that is rarer still. As on other ATC toys, the dual trademarks of ATC and Ichiko can be seen on the lid.

Although compact in its dimensions, the '58 Buick by Bandai is a very attractive model, further enhanced by the period artwork used on the box. *Courtesy of the Bruce Sterling Collection.* Price Category: 4

The Asahi version of the '58 Buick is extremely rare. *Courtesy of the Bruce Sterling Collection.* Price Category: 10

1959 Buicks

The excessive ornamentation of '58 Buicks gave way to sharp angles and tailfins the following year. The old names were out too, replaced by Invicta and Electra. Ichiko made a rare '59 Electra pictured here in red/white but also available in a much larger eighteen-inch size in green/white and maroon/white with extra chrome plating and door handles.

The cream and red remote-controlled car is of a similar vintage. The box carries the name of Cragstan, a well-known New York-based toy distributor of the time. Cragstan would buy in bulk from various Japanese makers but had a particularly close link with Yonezawa whose "Y" symbol frequently appears on boxes in addition to the Cragstan name. Diverse though they were, the one thing in common that early Cragstan lines had was the ingenuity of their mechanisms, one of the most famous being the "Crapshooter" figure who held a wad of dollars in one hand while he threw a dice with the other.

Similar ingenuity can be seen in Cragstan's remote control 1959 Buick, made for them by Nomura (TN). It comes with what is in effect a replica dashboard with steering wheel, shift lever for forward/reverse movement and operating horn button. (For another version of the TN Buick, see page 52). The car is around eleven inches long and has been seen in blue/white and silver/bronze as well as the yellow/red combination pictured.

1959 Buick by Ichiko. *Courtesy of the Bruce Sterling Collection.* Price Category: 7

Left: Cragstan's Remote-Control Buick. Right: The Ichiko version. *Courtesy of the Bruce Sterling Collection.* Price Category: 6 (Cragstan); 7 (Ichiko).

The box carries the name of the distributor Cragstan, whereas the actual manufacturer was TN. *Courtesy of the Bruce Sterling Collection.*

The most impressive feature of the Cragstan/TN model is the elaborate hand control unit, which is a dashboard in miniature. *Courtesy of the Bruce Sterling Collection.*

Reverse side of the hand control unit. *Courtesy of the Bruce Sterling Collection.*

Chevrolet

"New Look! New Life! New Everything!" ran the sales slogan for the 1955 Chevrolet. That wasn't entirely advertising hype: the new 265 cubic inch V8 engine really was a landmark, while the styling was fresh and original, making use of fashionable two-toning effects with the roof colour "splashing down" to the rear of the body.

The Japanese tin replica of the Chevrolet is something of a landmark, too. Marusan's Buick may not quite have equalled the standard of its Cadillac, but the Chevrolet came very close. This toy is even rarer than the Cadillac, one reason being that it is hardly ever found complete with its cable and control box. Battery-operated cars were often somewhat fragile and unreliable; once they had ceased to operate properly there would be little point in keeping the clumsy cable attached. Even collectors have been known to remove the cable as it makes the toy awkward to display on the shelf.

Top: Marusan's incredibly rare 1955 Chevrolet is usually found unboxed with the control box removed. *Courtesy of the Bruce Sterling Collection.* Price Category: 12

Bottom: This side view of the Marusan Chevrolet shows the detailed interior and gives a glimpse of the driver. *Courtesy of the Bruce Sterling Collection.*

Opening doors were an extremely unusual feature on Japanese tin toys of this vintage. *Courtesy of the Bruce Sterling Collection.*

However, the example shown here is complete. This is an unusual toy as it has opening doors, which reveal an exceptionally detailed lithographed interior, complete with driver. Cream with a green roof is believed to be the only colour scheme for this 10.5-inch model.

Note that the box doesn't identify this as a Chevrolet but simply calls it a "Nice Car." And who could disagree?

The other Chevrolet is an 8-inch 1963 Impala Coupe from Haji and it, too, has opening doors. This allowed further detail to be added to the door panels and seats, which are made separately, unlike most tin cars which have a single lithographed piece to represent the whole interior. The box description "Door-Matic Car Series" indicates that the Chevrolet is not the only car to have this feature; the series also includes a Ford Thunderbird and Buick Riviera.

A later Chevrolet, the 1963 Impala, comes from Haji's "Door-Matic" Series. *Courtesy of the Bruce Sterling Collection.* Price Category: 3

Interior fittings in tin toys were generally a single sheet of lithographed tinplate; in the Haji, like the 1955 Marusan, the seats are separate components. *Courtesy of the Bruce Sterling Collection.*

Oldsmobiles

There were so many chrome strips on the bodywork of the 1958 Oldsmobile Dynamic 88 that one car stylist of the time made fun of a picture of it by drawing a treble clef and some music notes on the rear fenders. All these chrome lines were faithfully reproduced by HTC on their twelve-inch model of the two-door hardtop. Unfortunately, the quality of the plating was suspect and it has usually lost its shine, making genuinely mint items very hard to find. This must be one of the few Japanese tin toys where the picture on the box actually shows the car inside!

The scarce 1958 Oldsmobile by HTC faithfully reproduces the excessive chrome strips that covered the body-work of the real car. *Courtesy of the Bruce Sterling Collection.* Price Category: 9.

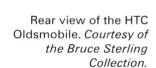

Rear view of the HTC Oldsmobile. *Courtesy of the Bruce Sterling Collection.*

Not as accurate, perhaps, but impressively large, is Yonezawa's 16.5-inch model of an Oldsmobile of the same vintage, always found in orange/cream with friction drive and sometimes with a driver in blue sporting a bow-tie. Placed beside the HTC model, the bulk of the Yonezawa is obvious.

Both these Oldsmobiles are friction powered but the HTC also came in an elaborate battery-operated Police version. The hand controller clipped on to the rear of the car and was attached by a length of cable. According to the instructions on the box, "when control button is pushed, patrol car stops and picture of driver appears on screen together with signal sounds." The roof light lit up as well. Obviously realism was sacrificed for play value on this one, but it is an interesting example of the increasing technical sophistication of Japanese tin toys.

Yonezawa's larger, if not totally accurate, 1958 Oldsmobile. *Courtesy of the Bruce Sterling Collection.* Price Category: 11

HTC Oldsmobile (left) with the Yonezawa (right). Note the driver in the larger car. *Courtesy of the Bruce Sterling Collection.*

The later "Highway Patrol" version of the HTC Oldsmobile with its curious hand control. *Courtesy of the Bruce Sterling Collection.* Price Category: 7

Front view of the two HTC Oldsmobiles. *Courtesy of the Bruce Sterling Collection.*

The other Oldsmobile is of even greater significance in this respect. One of the problems with remote-control cars was the need for a connecting cable, which restricted the car's movements. The "Radicon" remote control Oldsmobile was an early attempt to get around this problem.

The "Radicon" Oldsmobile claimed to be the "first and only" radio-controlled toy car. *Courtesy of the Bruce Sterling Collection.* Price Category: 7

Rear view of the Radicon Oldsmobile. *Courtesy of the Bruce Sterling Collection.*

Power was transmitted from an antenna on the control box to a similar aerial fitted on the bonnet, with batteries kept in a compartment on the base of the car and in the controller. No doubt the concept worked well enough, but whoever was the original purchaser of the example pictured here never tested it out: everything is perfectly mint and the aerials are still tied onto the cardboard inner packaging!

"Radicon" is presumably no more than a contraction of the words "radio" and "control" and the name was used on a "wireless remote control robot" which Masudaya made in 1958, which makes it seem likely that the Oldsmobile was a Masudaya product too. The concept was applied to other models such as a Mercedes 230SL and a single-deck bus.

At eleven inches long and seven inches wide the big Oldsmobile might not be the most elegant of tin toys, but it's certainly a significant piece. For one thing, there aren't all that many models of 1950s Oldsmobiles around, and toymakers tend to go for coupes and two-door sedans rather than four-door ones. In terms of the history of the remote-control car, the Radicon Oldsmobile is very much a transitional model: it combines traditional tinplate construction methods with the more modern radio-control technology. As such, the Radicon model offers a foretaste of developments to come—a whole new hobby, in fact: radio-control model cars.

1955–57 Fords

The years 1955–57 were good ones for Ford: the two-seater Thunderbird was a big success; the company was earning record profits; *Motor Trend* selected Ford as "Car of the Year" in 1956 and the following year Fords outsold market leader Chevrolet.

Classic car fans rate the mid-fifties Fords as being among the most stylish American cars of the period. These cars seemed to bring out the best in the Japanese toymakers too, for the Fords made by Bandai, Marusan, Yonezawa and Haji rank as near-perfect scale replicas—something that can't be said about every Japanese tin toy.

Bandai

Taking these in chronological order, Bandai's convertible is based on a 1955 Sunliner—even though the picture of the green and white car on the box is misleading as it depicts a 1957 model. The Bandai, which is 11.75 inches in length, has some novel operating features like the opening trunk lid, complete with a hinged strut, and tipping front seat backs. Its most remarkable feature is surely the exceptionally colourful lithographed interior: carpet pattern, window winders, dashboard instruments, foot pedals. . .nothing has been overlooked.

Bandai's 1955 Ford Sunliner is contained in a box which depicts a later model. *Courtesy of the Bruce Sterling Collection.* Price Category: 7

This rear view of the Bandai Sunliner shows the high quality of interior lithography. Even the lining of the luggage compartment is represented. *Courtesy of the Bruce Sterling Collection.*

It was a simple matter for Bandai to create other models using the convertible base, such as a pickup truck, estate car and delivery van. Strictly speaking, the grille appears to be that of the 1955 model while the chrome side flash resembles the one fitted on 1956 cars. The estate car and van have a rear door which opens in two sections, the glazed portion fold-ing upwards and the tailgate downwards, aided, once more, by a hinged strut. The estate car also came in white as an Ambulance. A boxed set en-titled "Ford Suburban Fleet" was marketed by the American toy distributor Cragstan and contained the pickup, convertible and estate car.

The "Flower Delivery Van" is essentially the same as the estate car with the side windows being blanked out by a panel reading "Flowers for Gracious Living." There is also a door insert depicting an elephant and the slogan "Ford Lasts Longer." This is the rarest version of the Bandai Ford and it's not difficult to see why it is so sought after. A pristine, boxed example has been known to command more than $1500.

It should also be noted that TN (Nomura) made another version of the estate car, based on the 1956 eight-passenger Ford Country Sedan. This again has opening rear doors and an unusual transparent yellow plastic roof panel running the entire length of the car. TN rather liked transparent roofs: they also made a Thunderbird with a clear plastic top. The inspiration no doubt came from the Plexiglass roof insert fitted to the real Ford Fairlane Crown Victoria.

The exquisitely decorated Flower Delivery Van is deservedly one of the most sought-after of all Bandai's tinplate toys. *Courtesy of the Bruce Sterling Collection.* Price Category: 10

Rear view of the Flower Van, showing the door which opens in two sections. *Courtesy of the Bruce Sterling Collection.*

Marusan

The mention of the Crown Victoria brings us to one of the very finest of Japanese tin toys—the 1956 Crown Victoria by Marusan. This model is not always accurately described: it carries a license plate which reads "1957" but there's no doubt the car is a 1956 model. It's usually called a "Crown Victoria" but lacks the forward-raked chrome roof band (sometimes called a "basket handle") associated with that car. The Marusan could, in fact, represent a two-door Fairlane Club Sedan.

Be that as it may, there can be no argument that this is a perfectly proportioned tin toy. It can have either friction or electric power, the batteries being carried in a compartment underneath providing sufficient power not only to move the car but to illuminate the front and rear lights as well. The model is always in two-tone colours, white with either red, blue, yellow, or pink.

The fabulously rare 1956 Ford from Marusan is as near to a perfect scale replica that can be found in the tinplate medium. *Courtesy of the Bruce Sterling Collection.* Price Category: 13

Rear view of the Marusan Ford. *Courtesy of the Bruce Sterling Collection.*

Yonezawa

Fractionally smaller than the thirteen-inch Marusan was the Yonezawa model, again in friction or electric versions, the latter with cable-operated remote control. It's not as good as the Marusan; it is made of thinner metal and the proportions are not quite right, particularly around the cabin area which seems too small. Nevertheless, this is still Yonezawa's most coveted tin toy. The car is usually

found not only in two-tone, but three-tone colour schemes, such as orange/turquoise/red roof and the red/white/dark blue roof shown here.

The Ford remained in production until at least 1964, as it is depicted in Yonezawa's trade catalogue for that year under reference number 9360, described as a "Golden Ford" which had "gold" rather than "chrome" trim.

Yonezawa's model of the same car came with either a friction motor or a battery-operated hand controller. *Courtesy of the Bruce Sterling Collection.* Price Category: 11

A comparison of the Yonezawa (left) with the Marusan (right) shows that the two models are far from identical. *Courtesy of the Bruce Sterling Collection.*

Haji

If Marusan and Yonezawa favoured the '56 Ford in hard top form, Haji preferred to go for the convertible. All three cars are inevitably similar in appearance, but they're put together in different ways. The Marusan has a one-piece lower body pressing and a separate roof section; on the Yonezawa and the Haji, however, the coloured body sides are separate sections from the upper half, the side body moulding covering over the join.

The Haji is friction-powered and comes in red/white or two-tone blue. Like the makers of the other two '56 Fords, Haji freely borrowed from Ford advertisements to create the box artwork. The Haji emblem printed on the reverse of the front seats is a nice touch. Haji liked the Ford so much that they made it twice over, both in 11.5- and 7.5-inch lengths, the smaller one being simpler and less realistic. Haji rarely reached the heights scaled by other brands like Asahi, Marusan and Alps, but the Ford is definitely their masterpiece.

This convertible version of the '56 Ford is considered to be the finest model to appear under the Haji name. *Courtesy of the Bruce Sterling Collection.* Price Category: 11

The "Haji" logo appears on the back of the seats of the Ford. *Courtesy of the Bruce Sterling Collection.*

The Haji Ford looks equally impressive in blue or red. *Courtesy of the Bruce Sterling Collection.*

Ford for '57

Fords were completely restyled for 1957; the fins at the back grew bigger, the headlamps at the front were aggressively hooded, and the wrap round windshield wrapped round even more in the "dog-leg" style. The motoring public liked the new design, as Ford built a record 1.67 million cars that model year, outselling their rival Chevrolet.

As they had done for the 1955 model, Bandai made twelve-inch models of '57 Fords in convert-ible, estate car and pick-up form, again fitted with an opening boot or tailgate and, in the case of the convertible, tipping seats. There's also a very clean-looking 9.5-inch Fairlane Victoria hardtop possibly made by Ichiko and distributed by ATC, as both trademarks can be found on the box (ATC—the Asahi Trading Company—acted as a distributor as well as making its own toys).

The model is shown here in both orange/pink and two-tone blue with a box that depicts a four-door Fairlane Town Sedan, although the model is in fact a two-door hardtop. One box describes the car as "friction car with siren" even though it's not a police car.

In short, when it comes to tinplate models of 1955-57 Fords, the enthusiast is spoiled for choice. Few Japanese tin toys can equal the accuracy, build quality and vivid colours of these toys.

Operating features fitted to the Bandai 1955 Ford Convertible, like tipping seats and an opening trunk, reappeared on this 1957 model. *Courtesy of the Bruce Sterling Collection.* Price Category: 7

Numerous tin toys appeared under the simple description "New Ford". This is the Ichiko Fairlane hardtop, shown in two different colour schemes. *Courtesy of the Bruce Sterling Collection.* Price Category: 5

In comparison, the '58 Ford, which comes in a box with the trademark "HTC", is something of an anti-climax. "Never judge the toy by the picture on the box" is a lesson that the collector of Japanese tin learns very quickly, and it certainly applies in this case. The toy does have the double headlamps fitted to the real car so tastefully pictured on the box lid; unfortunately the rest of it could be almost any fifties automobile. Those "stuck on" tailfins don't help either!

This 1958 Ford, marked HTC, suffers from heavy-handed treatment of the rear fins. *Courtesy of the Bruce Sterling Collection.* Price Category: 4

1960 Fords

"New" must have been the most overused word in the American automobile industry throughout the 1950s. Admittedly, the 1960 Ford line was very different from the previous year's, with softer, more curved styling appearing on the whole range, from the compact Falcon to the "full-size" Fairlane and Galaxie. Inevitably, then, when Haji brought out a model of a Sunliner convertible, they called it a "New Ford." Closer inspection, however, reveals that only some of it was new. The front and rear end styling are reasonably accurate, but the superstructure, with the old "dog-leg" windshield, came from the 1958 Edsel (see page 50). Marusan, too, did something similar, using common components to make models of the 1960 Ford and Chevrolet.

1960 Ford by Haji. A comparison of the model with the box illustration shows various discrepancies, particularly around the screen area. *Courtesy of the Bruce Sterling Collection.* Price Category: 6

The Sunliner might not be Haji's most realistic model, but it did have a clever feature that would appeal to children: not only did the hood lift to reveal a detailed engine, but there was a rotating cooling fan in plastic.

Haji also made a smaller (eight-inch) Ford Sunliner which looks similar at first glance but is based on a 1961 model. It is shown here with a caravan trailer, complete with table and chairs and opening awning, which rather overshadows the car. As so often with tin toys, the box illustrations of both these Haji toys do not reflect what's inside. The larger car comes in a box showing a Fairlane sedan while the "House Trailer" set depicts a '59 convertible.

A different sort of 1960 Ford comes from ATC: a twelve-inch station wagon in black and yellow "Standard Coffee" livery. Here again, it seems, savings were made by using an already-existing windscreen as on the Haji model. There are other inaccuracies too—the whole shape looks very flat and angular— but this does not alter the fact that this is perhaps the rarest of all Japanese tin models of American delivery vans. As for the box, it is practically unobtainable.

1960 Ford by Haji. A close-up of the rotating cooling fan. *Courtesy of the Bruce Sterling Collection.*

This 1961 Ford is also by Haji and comes with a House Trailer—complete with furniture. *Courtesy of Douglas R. Kelly.* Price Category: 6

1960 Ford Delivery Van by ATC in the rare "Standard Coffee" livery. *Courtesy of the Bruce Sterling Collection.* Price Category: 10/11

Lincolns

Although it is often described as a "Lincoln Continental," experts on the history of the American Ford company will know that the 1956 Continental Mark II was not actually marketed under the Lincoln name, as Ford tried to establish the car as a separate prestige brand. In these days of fussy styling relying heavily on masses of chrome plating, the classic lines of the Continental were remarkably clean and restrained. Everybody recognised its elegance—but that didn't mean they went out and bought one. Priced at $10,000, it is said that Ford lost $1,000 on every one they sold. Sadly, the Continental didn't last beyond 1957.

The 11.5-inch Linemar replica is remarkable in that it doesn't have the "chunky" feel of so many Japanese tin toys, capturing the long, low style of the real car perfectly. Particularly notable details are the accurate wheel trims, the spare wheel cover moulded into the boot lid, and the rear view mirror at the top of the windscreen frame. The bonnet mascot is an accurate replica of the Continental's badge, too—even though it might just be slightly out of scale!

There aren't many other tin cars as good as this one that can be positively identified as being by Linemar and the Continental is unquestionably their masterpiece. Only a handful of mint and boxed examples are known to survive in collections today. Most of these will be black, with light blue or maroon being even harder to find.

This battery-operated Continental by Linemar is very hard to find, especially with its original box. *Courtesy of the Bruce Sterling Collection.* Price Category: 12

The 1958 model was certainly not one of the better-looking cars to bear the Lincoln name. This 8.5-inch model is by Sanyo. *Courtesy of the Bruce Sterling Collection.* Price Category: 5

In addition to battery-operated forward and reverse movements, the Continental had electric front and rear lights. Such features appeared on many tin toys, of course, but when TN modeled a Lincoln Continental sedan they came up with something really novel: wheels that lit up! The box of the "Lite-o-Wheel" Lincoln shows a cartoon character lying on the ground beside the car reading by the light of the wheels, and no doubt this was a toy that children enjoyed playing with after dark when they were supposed to be asleep. Bizarre though this feature might be, it does not detract from the realism of the Lincoln as a model.

Many Japanese tin cars had electric lighting, but few had illuminating wheels! This Lincoln is by TN. *Courtesy of the Bruce Sterling Collection.* Price Category: 5

The TN "Lite-o-Wheel" Lincoln is shown with the much smaller diecast Cherryca Phenix model for comparison. *Courtesy of the Bruce Sterling Collection.*

The Lincoln Futura could hardly be more different from the restrained lines of the Continental. Although some pretty wild-looking cars did make it into production in America in the fifties, the Futura was simply a styling exercise, built in 1954-55 by Ghia, the Italian coachbuilders, to a design drawn up by Lincoln-Mercury stylists. It created quite a stir at various motor shows and in 1959 appeared in an MGM movie called *It Started with a Kiss* starring Glenn Ford and Debbie Reynolds.

The Lincoln Futura was a styling exercise rather than a production car. The model is by Alps. *Courtesy of the Bruce Sterling Collection.* Price Category: 10

Two versions of the Alps Lincoln: (left) the electric car and (right) the friction one. In both cases, the glazed canopy can be opened. *Courtesy of the Bruce Sterling Collection.*

The car was later purchased by Californian hot rod and custom car builder George Barris who supplied and modified vehicles for film use. After only three weeks in Barris' workshops, the Futura re-emerged with radically transformed black body-work, ready to star in the film *Batman*.

The original Futura might have been a one-off, but Alps managed to model it in three different versions: one with a friction drive mechanism (shown here in black); an electric one with an on/off switch at the rear and a battery compartment underneath and finally, the most elaborate of all, a remote-controlled model shown here in silver. This time the wheels were turned not by a steering wheel, but by a lever, and the forward/reverse buttons also switched on the lights. Note the completely different box styles used for each version. The futuristic glazed passenger canopy is hinged to allow a closer look at the colourful blue and cream interior. The most significant aspect of the model is the intricacy of its design, with the real car's multiple curves and fins all accurately pressed out of tin sheet.

The XL-500 was another "dream car" styling exercise from Ford's Lincoln-Mercury division. It had a fiberglass body and a completely glazed roof section—a feature that influenced production cars like the 1954 Mercury Sun Valley, which didn't sell very well as drivers complained that the interior was unbearably hot! The XL-500 was modeled, very accurately, in tin by Yonezawa—a remarkable achievement as the toy is only 7.5 inches long. Colours include blue, red, and yellow. As one would expect, the glazed canopy is easily cracked and perfect mint and boxed examples are so hard to find that they have been known to sell for as much as $1500.

Yonezawa made this model of the XL-500, another "dream car" styling exercise from Ford's Lincoln-Mercury division. *Courtesy of the Bruce Sterling Collection.* Price Category: 7

Rear view of the Yonezawa XL-500. *Courtesy of the Bruce Sterling Collection.*

the four different two-door 1958 Edsels—Citation, Corsair, Pacer and Ranger—the Haji model is usually said to represent the Corsair, although the shape of the roof and rear window are not very accurate. Being a two-door, the model was easily made into a convertible, the same box style being used in each case. Haji did an estate car, too, with an opening rear window and tailgate, also available in Ambulance livery.

Edsel

An early Edsel advertisement claimed that "there has never been a car like the Edsel." Most people would agree with that statement—though probably not for the reasons that Ford originally had in mind. The Edsel might have been a disaster during the brief time it was in production but it now has a healthy following among classic car enthusiasts. According to the highly informative web site of the Edsel Owners' Club, more than a hundred different tin toy Edsels have been recorded. Just two are shown here—but they're two of the best.

The bigger model is by Haji, a name we have already met in connection with the 1956 Ford. Of

This view shows how well-proportioned the Haji Edsels are. *Courtesy of the Bruce Sterling Collection.*

One thing guaranteed to upset an Edsel devotee is to refer to his favourite car as a "Ford Edsel," since it had been Ford's intention to establish Edsel as a separate range. Nevertheless, Fords and Edsels had many common parts and even in the first model year they were built alongside each other. The same thing must have been happening on the Haji toy production line as well: a comparison of the Edsel with the 1960 Ford pictured on page 43 shows that the roof pressing, interior fittings and even the base plate are shared by the two cars.

The Haji Edsel (background) with the smaller model by KTS in a box marked Lang Craft. *Courtesy of the Bruce Sterling Collection.* Price Category: 10 (Haji); 6 (KTS).

Opposite page, bottom right:
Two of the various Edsel models by Haji: convertible (left) and hardtop (right). *Courtesy of the Bruce Sterling Collection.* Price Category: 9/10

A comparison of the Haji Edsel with the 1960 Ford reveals that the same roof components have been used for each model. *Courtesy of the Bruce Sterling Collection.*

It often happens that smaller tin toys are less successful in capturing the lines of a car than larger ones. But there are exceptions to every rule, and the other '58 Edsel shown here is one. The extra detailing inside the "scalloped" section of the rear panel confirms that this represents a top of the range Edsel Citation. The shape of the roof line is accurately rendered and while the tin sheet is on the thin side there is a compensating delicacy in the the overall finish. Little is known about the background of this toy; the box states that the maker is KTS and also carries the name "Lang Craft," presumably the distributor.

Among the numerous other Edsels is a fine model of the Citation by Asahi. It had "gold" detailing to the grille and hood mascot and in terms of size it is nearer to the Haji version than the KTS.

The well-balanced profile of the KTS/Lang Craft model of the '58 Edsel. *Courtesy of the Bruce Sterling Collection.* Price Category: 6

Police Cars

Even a collector with no more than a casual interest in tin toys will have noticed that a disproportionately large number of these seem to be police cars. There are perhaps two reasons for this. One is that it was easy for a company to produce a "new" toy simply by recolouring an existing car in a police livery, thus saving the cost of new tooling. The second is that police cars offered more scope for "action" features that would appeal to children. The sound of a siren is an obvious example, even if this often amounted to little more than the noise that the friction mechanism would make anyway! Flashing roof lights were another popular feature.

The models shown here give an idea of how many variations could be achieved on the police patrol car theme. The first two examples, a Buick and Ford respectively, are friction-powered cars by Ichiko. Both have a roof light which does not actually illuminate but swivels from side to side as the car is pushed along. In order to fit the model into the box, this light is detachable and, inevitably, is often missing. Next comes a 12.5-inch 1963 Ford with battery-operated roof lights in a box marked

Taiyo. Fords were popular choices with many American police forces, but a Continental Mark II would have been a most unlikely pursuit vehicle. Nevertheless, KS made one, although it is hardly up to the standard of the Linemar version shown earlier. It comes with a remote control and flashing rooflight.

An eleven-inch Buick Highway Patrol Car by Ichiko, with a swivelling roof light mechanism fitted to many other tinplate police cars. *Courtesy of the Alex J. Cameron Collection.* Price Category: 3

A slightly smaller nine-inch Ichiko police car, based on a Ford and featuring the same roof light as the Buick. *Courtesy of the Alex J. Cameron Collection.* Price Category: 2

This patrol car by Taiyo is loosely based on a 1963 Ford and has a battery-powered roof light. *Courtesy of the Alex J. Cameron Collection.* Price Category: 3

The Continental Mark II was an unlikely vehicle for police use, but KS made this 9.5-inch model nevertheless. *Courtesy of the Bruce Sterling Collection.* Price Category: 5

The Buick by TN and the Oldsmobile by HTC were also discussed earlier, but are shown here again as examples of how variations of existing models could be created by changing the lithography to produce police cars.

The last two models, both Fords by Marusan, are particularly rare. One is an early fifties-style Ford, harder to find mint and boxed than the car in ordinary colours. This one is battery-operated and comes with a swivelling roof light—and a couple of police officers inside too! Note the twin trademarks on the box: San, denoting the manufacturer Marusan, and Cragstan, the distributor. This car can also be found in a yellow and red Taxi livery. The existence of the other model has only recently come to light: a 1956 Ford which is not simply a variation on Marusan's "famous" '56 Ford, but an entirely different, lithographed toy. Almost every detail is

lithographed on this one, even the roof lights and siren. Instead of window glazing there are pictures of two officers in the front and two in the back, one of whom is smoking a pipe. The 'San' trademark is present on both the box and the model, where it is lithographed on the left rear panel.

Bruce Sterling says of this model that it is "a wonderful experience to learn of and come across something 'new'—a discovery which once again awakens that feeling of wonder we all had long ago when we began collecting." With Japanese tin toys, the last word can never be written.

This friction Buick by TN is basically the same car as the remote-control one distributed by Cragstan. *Courtesy of the Bruce Sterling Collection.* Price Category: 4

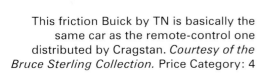

An Oldsmobile police car by HTC. For a description of how the toy works, see page 32. *Courtesy of the Bruce Sterling Collection.* Price Category: 7

Marusan's Ford patrol car—shown with a box carrying the name of the distributor, Cragstan—is considerably rarer than the civilian version of the same car. *Courtesy of the Bruce Sterling Collection.* Price Category: 6

This 1956 Ford police car, also by Marusan, is unusual in making greater use of lithography. *Courtesy of the Bruce Sterling Collection.* Price Category: 7

Close-up of the Marusan police car, showing the rear passengers and roof details. *Courtesy of the Bruce Sterling Collection.*

Kaiser Darrin Roadster

Towards the end of World War II ex-General Motors and Chrysler man Joe Frazer teamed up with shipbuilding magnate Henry J. Kaiser to form the Kaiser-Frazer Corporation. Kaiser-Frazer got off to a good start by putting a genuinely new car on sale in May 1946, ready to cash in on the post-war demand. Unfortunately, this early success proved to be short-lived and Kaiser-Frazer was struggling by 1953. Even so, Henry Kaiser was still willing to have a go at marketing a radical new design by stylist Howard "Dutch" Darrin—a fiberglass-bodied sports car with side doors that did not open in the usual way but slid into the front fenders. Sadly, only 435 were built.

Not the most obvious choice for a tin toy, but Ichiko made one—or rather two, for the model came in both 8.5- and 5.5-inch lengths. As so often, however, the smaller version was less accurate, especially when, as in this case, it came with a caricatured driver.

The 8.5-inch Darrin was powered electrically, the battery compartment inevitably intruding into the interior space. This was not a remote-control toy: it had a switch at the rear with forward-stop-reverse settings.

The drawing on the box might seem to flatter the car by elongating it but the real thing was in fact longer and lower than the toy would suggest, partly as a long front was needed to make space for the sliding doors, a feature not present on the toy.

This is a rare model, hardly ever seen with its box. As with several other toys already described, this one carries dual Ichiko/Asahi trademarks. And the curious description "Darlin 161"? The 161 is easily explained, as this was the official model number used by Kaiser-Frazer. Presumably the name "Darrin" was changed on the toy because permission to use it had been refused—or, more likely, because permission had never been sought in the first place.

The larger of the two versions of the Kaiser Darrin Roadster made by Ichiko. *Courtesy of the Bruce Sterling Collection.* Price Category: 6

This rear view of the Ichiko Darrin shows details of the lithographed interior. Note also the stop/go switch at the rear. *Courtesy of the Bruce Sterling Collection.*

Packard and Chrysler

While virtually any of the items pictured in this book could justifiably claim to be among the best of Japanese tinplate, there's a handful of toys that are so stunningly well-made and realistic that they stand apart from all the others. Marusan's Cadillac and Ford are universally agreed to belong to this select group. Two others with similar credentials are the Packard Patrician by Alps and the Chrysler Imperial by Asahi.

In the 1950s the Packard name no longer had quite the prestige it had carried in the Twenties and Thirties. The styling of some of the post-war models earned them unkind nicknames like "bathtub"

and "pregnant elephant,"' but 1951 saw the advent of a more modern look which lasted until the next restyle in '55.

The Alps model is based on a 1953 Patrician. This is a big toy—sixteen inches in length—with an unmistakable "presence." The interior is so well-lithographed that there's even a copy of *Life* magazine lying on the back shelf! The model can be found in "standard" or "deluxe" finish. Among the refinements of the deluxe version are a winged "cormorant" hood mascot, blacked-in detail on the grille, and whitewall tires, in addition to the beautifully accurate chrome hubs. The most common colour for the Packard is black, and it also came in bronze with a blue roof, but it looks best in red.

The sixteen-inch Alps Packard is one of the most imposing of all Japanese tinplate American cars. It is more often seen in black than red. *Courtesy of the Bruce Sterling Collection.* Price Category: 12

The "deluxe" finish of the Alps Packard included black detailing on the grille and a winged cormorant mascot. *Courtesy of the Bruce Sterling Collection.*

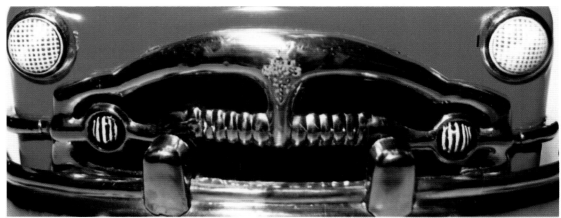

Magazines on the rear shelf of the Packard—a delightful touch. *Courtesy of the Bruce Sterling Collection.*

Of course, criticisms could be made. The door handle arrangement is incorrect and the chrome bumpers are so large that they almost extend to ground level. Alps also made a convertible in the usual manner, using the lower half of the sedan. While they did omit the rear door handles to give the effect of the proper two-door configuration, the shut lines of the back doors are still there.

All that is easily forgiven, though. Tin Packards are few and far between, and this one was never surpassed.

The ATC 1962 Chrysler Imperial is of similar length to the Packard but it is less bulky. The shape is complex—look at the indentations on the sides of the roof, for example, the correctly sloping rear deck, or the spaces behind the headlamps—but the sweeping proportions of the toy are just like the original. There are innumerable small details: mirrors, badges, mascot and the bizarre tail lights, but each has been perfectly rendered. Many tin toys suffer from heavy-handed detailing, particularly where chrome strips or window frames are concerned, with these components often being far too thick or attached with clumsy tabs. On the Chrysler, however, each piece of trim is a flawless fit.

Such a level of quality was never to be reached again in tinplate, and it is therefore fitting to end this survey of Japanese tin toys at this point. A specialist collector would have to pay dearly to add the Chrysler to his collection, though. In June 1999 one of the very few surviving examples of this toy sold at an auction in Germany for around $19,000.

Opposite page:
A page from a trade catalogue of ATC (Asahi) products lists the Imperial as a new addition to the range. Note the contrast between this quality item and the crude 8.5-inch Chevrolets pictured above it. *Courtesy of the Bruce Sterling Collection.*

Often considered the ultimate tin toy: the 1962 Chrysler Imperial from Asahi. *Courtesy of the Bruce Sterling Collection.* It has been known to sell for $19,000 or more.

This view of the Asahi Imperial shows the many separately applied tinplate details such as mirrors, door handles and badges. *Courtesy of the Bruce Sterling Collection.*

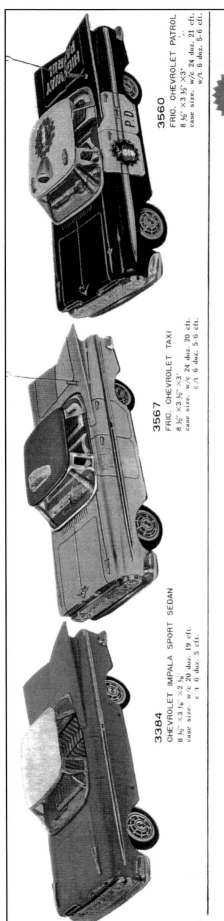

3384

CHEVROLET IMPALA SPORT SEDAN

8 ½″ × 3 ¾″ × 2 ⅜″

case size. w/c 20 doz. 19 cft.

c/t 6 doz. 5 cft.

3567

FRIC. CHEVROLET TAXI

8 ½″ × 3 ½″ × 3″

case size. w/c 24 doz. 20 cft.

c/t 6 doz. 5-6 cft.

3560

FRIC. CHEVROLET PATROL

8 ½″ × 3 ½″ × 3″

case size. w/c 24 doz. 21 cft.

w/t 6 doz. 5-6 cft.

3597

FRIC. CHRYSLER IMPERIAL

15 ¾″ × 6 ¼″ × 4 ¼″

case size. w/c 4 doze. 16-0 cft.

c/t 1 doz. 3-8 cft.

3598

FRIC. CHEVROLET IMPALA

11″ × 4 ¾″ × 4 ¼″

case size. w/c 8 doz. 18-5 cft.

c/t 2 doz. 4-2 cft.

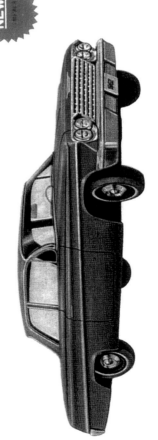

AUTHENTICALLY REPRODUCED STREAM LINERS —MODEL CARS !

ULTRA MODERN MODEL TOYS OF AMERICAN AUTOMOBILE !!

All those model toys are incorporated elegance and gorgeousness suitable for the name of deluxe model cars. Every model is full of fresh design, elegant style and authenticity.

NEW MODEL CAR

CHAPTER THREE

Tinplate European Cars

Bandai no. 743 was a Fiat 600, just one of the many interesting European cars this company chose to model. A novel feature is the sunroof which can slide backwards and forwards. *Courtesy of the Bruce Sterling Collection.* Price Category: 3

Introduction

Europe was the second biggest export market for Japanese tin toys and this is reflected in the number of tinplate models of European cars that were made. Germany, in particular, had a long tradition of tin toy manufacture, and the Japanese were quick to take advantage of the fact that the German toy industry had suffered badly during the second World War. Indeed, so successful was Japan in harnessing its labour force to produce large quantities of good quality tin toys at cheap prices that the German industry never managed to regain its former position. Tin toys were popular in Great Britain, too, made by such companies as Chad Valley, Wells-Brimtoy, and Mettoy (which had been founded by German businessmen who had left their home country to escape the Nazis). The sale of Japanese toys in Britain was limited by import restrictions but a perusal of toy trade journals of the period reveals that there were some distributors with Far Eastern connections who specialised in these lines, such as Codeg (short for Cowan de Groot) of Chart Street, London N1 or Libro of Brewer Street, W1 who are listed as being "importers of Japanese mechanical toys and sole importers for SSS of Tokyo." It is interesting to note, too, that the Japanese found it worth their while to produce toys in liveries which would have been for sale in only one European country, such as the "ADAC Strassenwacht" Volkswagen. Figures published in the British trade journal *Games and Toys* show that in the the course of 1961 Japan exported twelve million dollars' worth of toys to Europe.

However, Europe was not the only market for models of European cars. To help the regeneration of post-war economies, European car manufacturers made strenuous efforts to sell their cars in the USA, and some of these (especially British sports cars) sold well, so that tinplate models of the Jaguar XK120 or the MG would have been quite popular in America. Furthermore, some European cars were familiar on Japanese roads, too—such as certain Austins, Hillmans and Renaults which were built in Japan under license—so that the choice of these cars to model was a perfectly logical one.

Of all the various ranges of tin cars, the one with the most international flavour was Bandai's "Automobiles of the World" series. A deliberate attempt was made to be representative, resulting in an impressively wide inventory covering not only Rolls Royce, Citroen, Ferrari, Mercedes-Benz, and Volkswagen, but

also cars that were comparatively less well-known outside their country of origin, like the DKW 1000 or Zuendapp Janus from Germany, the MG Magnette from Britain, and the Swedish Saab. The Bandai leaflet reproduced here shows some of the range, and others are discussed in more detail later in this chapter. Again, only a selection of the models that were available can be illustrated here, but they're undoubtedly among the very best.

This Volvo 1800ES from Ichiko shows that Japanese toy makers often selected unusual vehicles to model. This is a fairly late example of a tinplate toy, probably dating from the early 1970s. *Courtesy of the Bruce Sterling Collection.*
Price Category: 5

This leaflet supplied with a Bandai model illustrates a small selection of the "Automobiles of the World" series, drawn from Great Britain, Italy, Germany, Sweden, Japan as well as the U.S.A. Note the claims made for the superior quality of Bandai's friction motor!

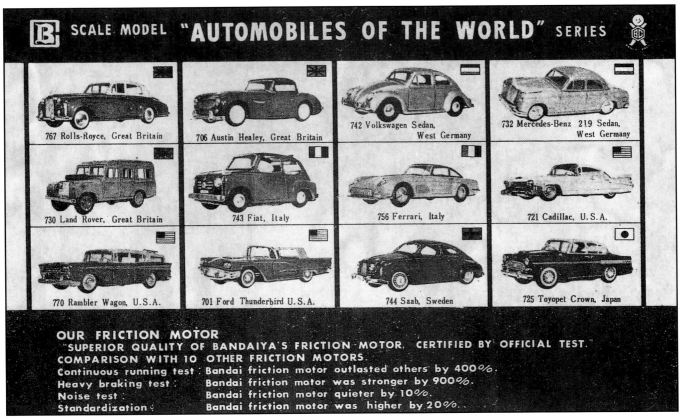

B SCALE MODEL "AUTOMOBILES OF THE WORLD" SERIES

767 Rolls-Royce, Great Britain

706 Austin Healey, Great Britain

742 Volkswagen Sedan, West Germany

732 Mercedes-Benz 219 Sedan, West Germany

730 Land Rover, Great Britain

743 Fiat, Italy

756 Ferrari, Italy

721 Cadillac, U.S.A.

770 Rambler Wagon, U.S.A.

701 Ford Thunderbird U.S.A.

744 Saab, Sweden

725 Toyopet Crown, Japan

OUR FRICTION MOTOR
"SUPERIOR QUALITY OF BANDAIYA'S FRICTION MOTOR, CERTIFIED BY OFFICIAL TEST."
COMPARISON WITH 10 OTHER FRICTION MOTORS.
Continuous running test : Bandai friction motor outlasted others by 400%.
Heavy braking test : Bandai friction motor was stronger by 900%.
Noise test : Bandai friction motor quieter by 10%.
Standardization : Bandai friction motor was higher by 20%.

British Cars

Jaguars and Rolls Royces

Great Britain used to have a motor industry to be proud of. Today famous names like Austin, Morris, Humber, and Hillman have all disappeared, and the remaining volume car makers—Rover, Vauxhall, even Jaguar—are all branches of much bigger multinational groupings.

Import restrictions meant that few British cars found their way to Japan in the fifties and sixties, but the prestige of some British marques was such that it was inevitable that tin replicas would emerge. The Jaguar XK120, for instance, was the most glamorous of British post-war sports cars and a replica of it was made by MT, the same firm that made the Renault 4CV (see page 69). The 4CV was not the most realistic tin toy ever made, and MT's Jaguar was arguably even less so. It's much too squat in appearance and doesn't really capture the sweeping curves of the original. To be honest, it bears only a tenuous resemblance to a Jaguar—which is perhaps why MT just described it as a "sports car." Still, the box picture with the palm trees is rather nice.

A Jaguar XK120 by MT. *Courtesy of the Bruce Sterling Collection.* Price Category: 3

A page from an Asahi trade catalogue showing a selection of European sports cars.

3574
FRIC. M. G. "A" OPEN
9 ½" × 3 ¾" × 2 ¾"
case size. w/c 18 doz. 18 cft.
c/t 4 doz. 3·6 cft.

3562
FRIC. M. G. "A" SEDAN
9 ½" × 3 ¾" × 3"
case size. w/c 18 doz. 19·5 cft.
c/t 4 doz. 4·0 cft.

3573
FRIC. KARMANN GHIA
9 ½" × 3 ¾" × 3"
case size. w/c 18 doz. 19·5 cft.
c/t 4 doz. 4·0 cft.

SPORTS CAR

Japan's Best Quality
SCALE MODEL TOY EUROPEAN CARS

Carefully made according to specifications obtained from the European makers of each of the various models. Japan's highest quality metal toys of this type. Now known throughout the world for their authentic detail, durability and excellent finish.

3583
FRIC. RENAULT FLORIDE SEDAN
9 ½" × 3 ¾" × 3"
case size. w/c 18 doz. 19·5 cft.
c/t 4 doz. 4·0 cft.

3557
RENAULT FLORIDE
With removable hyzex made top and specially painted seat
9 ½" × 3 ¾" × 3"
case size. w/c 18 doz. 21 cft.
c/t 4 doz. 4·2 cft.

3575
FRIC. FERARRI
9 ½" × 3 ¾" × 3"
case size. w/c 18 doz. 19·5 cft.
c/t 4 doz. 4·0 cft.

There are other similarly caricatured XK120s around: one is trademarked "KO," and another, by Bandai, is brightly coloured in red, blue, and yellow to represent an Indianapolis car. Bandai also made a much more realistic open-top version while Yonezawa's eight-inch replica of the same car (shown here in a catalogue reproduction) captures the low, sleek lines of the Jaguar very successfully.

The XK 120 evolved into the XK 150, looking much more modern without the split windshield and covered-in rear wheels of its predecessor. Bandai modelled this car too, and went on to make the XKE (E Type) which replaced it. Bandai also made nu-merous other British roadsters like the Lotus Elite, MGTF and MGA.

Almost every range of toy cars has included a replica of the Rolls-Royce, universally regarded as "the best car in the world," and the Japanese tin toy industry was no exception. The Silver Cloud, in production from 1955 onwards, was the most frequently chosen prototype, and three different examples are shown here for comparison.

The gray car is believed to be a Haji product; if it is indeed from this stable, it is not up to the standard of Haji's masterpieces like their 1956 Ford convertible. Being only six inches long, though, the Rolls could not be expected to have the same level of detail.

This catalogue illustration of Yonezawa's version of the Jaguar reveals it to be better proportioned than the MT model.

# 4520	JAGUAR SPORTS CAR (Friction)
Size;	8" × 2¾" × 2⅜"
Packing;	Each in Box.
	Export Packing.
	Carton case- 6dozen of 3'-5"
	Wooden case-24dozen of 16'
Net Weight; 2.9kg. (Per doz)	

Bandai's Silver Cloud is twice as long but is similarly constructed, with the superstructure being a separate component. This has two advantages; it was easy to create two-tone colour schemes, and the car could also be produced as a convertible simply by leaving off the upper section. The fact that Rolls Royce didn't actually make a four-door Silver Cloud convertible didn't seem to matter!

This six-inch Rolls Royce Silver Cloud is marked with the letters HTC. *Courtesy of the Bruce Sterling Collection.* Price Category: 1

A far greater level of detail was possible on Bandai's larger Rolls Royce. As the upper and lower sections are separate tinplate pressings, it was a simple matter for Bandai to produce two-tone colour schemes. Nevertheless the all-black version can command as much as twice the price of the commoner two-tone one. *Courtesy of the Bruce Sterling Collection.* Price Category: 5 (two-tone); 7 (all black).

The Bandai shown here is a rare variation as it is in all-over black, which flatters the model as the gap between the top and bottom halves is less noticeable.

The black livery, combined with the nicely lithographed wheel hubs and whitewall tires, gives the Bandai a dignified air, but the TN model is better still. There are no markings on the model itself, so that even the Kelley and Kitahara books list it as unidentified, but on the rare occasions where the box is present the letters "TN" in a lozenge-shaped logo can be found in the right hand corner, identifying the source of this model as the Nomura Toy company.

The drawing on the box for the Rolls Royce is typical of the style used on other Bandai "Automobiles of the World." *Courtesy of the Bruce Sterling Collection.*

This Rolls Royce with electric lights is another less common version of the Bandai. Note the completely different box design. *Courtesy of the Bruce Sterling Collection.* Price Category: 7

A comparison of the TN Rolls Royce (left) with the Bandai (right). *Courtesy of the Bruce Sterling Collection.* Price Category: 6 (TN)

The real car came out in 1955, originally with a six-cylinder engine, giving way to the V8 Silver Cloud II in 1959. In 1962 the Mark III acquired double headlamps. As the TN model has single lights and "1960" on the license plate, it is safe to assume that it represents a Silver Cloud II.

The friction-powered model came in duotone colours such as gray over pale bronze or two-tone blue. Just in case the purchaser didn't realise it was a Rolls Royce, the name is embossed underneath in a huge flowing script. The electric version tends to be single-coloured and the writing on the base-plate is replaced by a swivelling "stop and go" mechanism. According to the box, this gives the car a "mystery action"—"when it hits an obstacle it sounds horn and tail-lights glow." Both lack interior fittings and have dark blue tinted windows to conceal the mechanism inside. But there are some subtle differences between the two: one car has two small vents beneath the headlamps but no Spirit of Ecstasy mascot. The mascot on the silver car is made of tin, unlike that of the Bandai which is plastic—much to the dismay of purists.

Note the slight differences in frontal detail between the battery-operated version of the TN Rolls Royce (left) and the friction model (right). *Courtesy of the Bruce Sterling Collection.*

There's little doubt that the TN model is unsurpassed among tinplate Silver Clouds. It is, quite simply, the Rolls Royce of Rolls Royce models.

Side view of the two TN Rolls Royces: battery (left) and friction (right). *Courtesy of the Bruce Sterling Collection.*

British Family Cars

Cars like the Austin Cambridge and Hillman Minx would seem to be as British as Buckingham Palace or the Houses of Parliament . . . except that they were built in Japan as well as England.

After the Second World War the Japanese lacked the resources to develop and mass-produce their own cars. The British, on the other hand, were churning out as many as they could build but found that import restrictions hampered their attempts to sell cars in Japan. The solution to both problems lay in agreements between British and Japanese car companies that allowed British cars to be assembled in Japan under license. These deals were negotiated between Austin and Nissan and between the Rootes Group and Isuzu.

This background explains why the tinplate Austin and Hillman cars shown here came to be made. The Austin is based on a car which first appeared in 1954 as the A40 Cambridge, soon to be followed by the larger-engined A50. This remained in production until 1957 when it was replaced by the A55, easily distinguished by its longer boot and larger rear window.

Two different colour schemes on the scarce KS Austin A50 Cambridge, a very British-looking car which was nevertheless assembled in Japan. *Courtesy of the Bruce Sterling Collection.* Price Category: 8

The box of the Cambridge carries a discreet logo containing the letter "K" against a cloverleaf background, believed to be the trademark of Kokyu Shokai. Individual components like the "Flying A" bonnet mascot, side flashes, and radio aerial are a tribute to the accuracy of the model.

The friction-driven Austin is known to exist in dark green, red, and blue, all with a contrasting white roof. There's also a smaller tin replica of the car made in a style which is so similar to the larger one that it is almost certainly from the same manufacturer.

Rear view of the two Austins: the date "1959" on the license plate presumably refers to the year the model was produced. *Courtesy of the Bruce Sterling Collection.*

This close-up of the front of the Austin shows the numerous small tin pressings which would all have been fitted by hand. Note particularly the "Flying A" emblem characteristic of Austins of the period. *Courtesy of the Bruce Sterling Collection.*

Austin's links with Nissan go back to the 1930s but it was not until 1953 that the agreement between Rootes and Isuzu led to the Hillman Minx becoming visible on Japanese roads. This inspired Yonezawa to model the 1948–56 Minx, shown here in red. At around seven inches in length the

A scarce early post-war Hillman Minx by Yonezawa. *Courtesy of the Bruce Sterling Collection.* Price Category: 6

Yonezawa is signficantly smaller than most of the tinplate cars discussed in this book but it still manages to get the proportions of the real car right. A larger and more modern body style with a wrap-around rear window replaced the earlier design in 1956. As was common at the time, the Rootes Group regularly facelifted their cars; by 1959 the Minx had sprouted unusual curved tailfins and it was this car that Bandai chose to model.

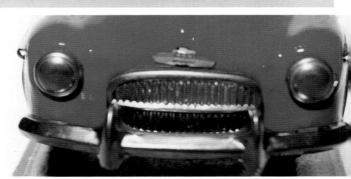

The box of the Minx is a work of art in itself. The coat of arms seems so traditionally British that one would never guess this was a Japanese product! *Courtesy of the Bruce Sterling Collection.*

Yonezawa Hillman (rear view). *Courtesy of the Bruce Sterling Collection.*

Yonezawa Hillman (front view). *Courtesy of the Bruce Sterling Collection.*

The provenance of the Austin Cambridge might have been rather obscure, but there's no difficulty in identifying the Minx as a Bandai product, for this beautifully preserved example still has the original cardboard tag showing the "B" logo of the company. The Minx is 10.5 inches long—larger than the Cambridge—and again comes in two-tone colours such as red/white and green/white. Note that the white upper section of the body incorporates the boot lid and rear wings as well as the roof.

A later Hillman Minx, modelled by Bandai. The condition of this item is so pristine that it even has the original cardboard tag attached. *Courtesy of the Bruce Sterling Collection.* Price Category: 7

Close up of the front grille of the Bandai Minx. *Courtesy of the Bruce Sterling Collection.*

This figure, and the stylised letter "B", can be found on most Bandai products of the 1960s. The letter "B" is generally present on the underside of the tinplate cars, making Bandai models the most straightforward to identify. *Courtesy of the Bruce Sterling Collection.*

The desirability of the Yonezawa Hillman and the Austin Cambridge is further increased by the high standard of the box artwork, which despite its Far Eastern origins has an authentic English feel to it—inspired, as so often, by skillful imitation of the style of illustration to be found in contemporary car advertising literature.

French Cars

Citroen 2CV and DS19

They're both Citroens, but there could hardly be two cars that look less like each other than the DS and 2CV. One is elegant and futuristic; the other plain and utilitarian. The French name for one resembles the word *déesse* (meaning "goddess"); the other was nicknamed the *parapluie à roulettes* (meaning "umbrella on roller-skates").

So many tinplate, diecast and plastic replicas of these cars exist that a whole book could be written about them. In fact, it already has: the *Encyclopédie des Jouets Citroen* by Marc Hermans and Fabien Sabatès, who list no fewer than 588 models of the 2CV and 600 of the DS. Obviously, most of these are French in origin, but the two from Japan pictured here would certainly rank among the "must haves" for a serious Citroen collector.

Like many other Japanese tin toys, the 2CV goes under more than one trademark. The box carries a diamond-shaped logo with the word "Hoku" but the maker is actually Daiya. This 1/15 scale model is friction-driven and

Daiya's Citroen 2CV has delicate headlamps which are often missing on unboxed examples. *Courtesy of the Bruce Sterling Collection.* Price Category: 5

has one unusual feature: the rear axle is fitted to what the box calls a "spring cushion" to mimic the bouncy ride of the real car. Pristine examples are few and far between; the colourful box depicting the Eiffel Tower and a pavement cafe is hard to find, while unboxed examples tend to have broken or missing headlamps. Known colours include red, maroon and blue-gray, all with a separate roof section painted cream.

The Citroen DS is by Bandai, no. 739 in the "Automobiles of the World" series. It' s about twelve inches long and is made with impressive attention to detail—particularly that lithographed leopard-skin interior. Presumably the model dates from 1960 or soon after, as it was in that year that the strange air vents were fitted to the top of the front fenders.

The box of the Citroen carries a variety of different names and code numbers, presumably referring to distributors. Note the French pavement café with the Eiffel Tower in the background. *Courtesy of the Bruce Sterling Collection.*

This 12-inch Citroen is the larger of the two from Bandai. The leopard-skin interior is particularly effective. *Courtesy of the Bruce Sterling Collection.* Price Category: 7

A close up of the lithographed dash showing the "Double Chevron" emblem used by Citroen. *Courtesy of the Bruce Sterling Collection.*

This beautiful orange and cream example is just one of numerous Citroens from Bandai. It came in colours such as red/white and blue/white, and battery as well as friction-powered cars were available. There were also the smaller, eight-inch versions, available in saloon, convertible, and ID 19 estate car form. Someone at Bandai must have been a Citroen fan.

Rear view of the 2CV (left) and the DS (right). *Courtesy of the Bruce Sterling Collection.*

Renault 4CV

The Renault 4CV did for post-war France what the Model T Ford did for the United States and the Austin Seven for Great Britain: it made motoring a possibility for ordinary people. Yet the little rear-engined Renault was a familiar sight on the roads of Tokyo as well as in Paris, since the terms of a 1953 licensing agreement with the Hino Diesel Company allowed it to be assembled in Japan.

There are two known Japanese tinplate models of the 4CV, similar in size (around 7.5 inches) but very different in style. One carries the logo "MT" which stands for "Modern Toys," the actual maker being Masudaya. Note the difference between the grille patterns on the gray and green cars. One has three chrome strips as fitted to the French car from 1954 onwards, whereas the other has the full length grille of the Hino-Renault. It seems likely, then, that different versions were made for the home (Japanese) and export markets. The model can have either a friction or electric motor, the latter being operated by a very visible lever which sticks out on the left hand side.

Two versions of the Masudaya Renault 4CV. The green car (left) is friction powered whereas the gray one (right) is electric. There are also differences in box design and in the style of the front grilles. *Courtesy of the Bruce Sterling Collection.* Price Category: 6 (electric); 4 (friction).

First impressions are that the MT Renault is not a very good likeness of the real thing: the shape seems too flat, the wheels don't fit into the wheel arches very well and the front and rear bumpers stick out too much. The gray car even has green bumper supports, suggesting that there was a surplus of green components and the factory just used them up without bothering to repaint them. On the other hand, attention to detail can be seen at the rear of the model where the engine louvres have all been cut out separately. There are exactly nine on each side, just like the real car.

This close-up shows the three-bar grille fitted on French-built cars after 1954. *Courtesy of the Bruce Sterling Collection.*

On the electric Renault, the batteries are inserted in a compartment underneath the car. *Courtesy of the Bruce Sterling Collection.*

In spite of the French description "Bon Renault," this box depicts the Japanese-built Hino-Renault car. *Courtesy of the Bruce Sterling Collection.*

The second model, by Yonezawa, captures the shape much more successfully. The car is shown in various colours, all of them being fitted with the Hino grille, but there are some minor differences; the blue car has separate door handles and front indicator lights. Both have a wing mirror, correctly placed on the right-hand side as Japanese cars, like British ones, are right-hand drive. The only problem is that the Yonezawa has its steering wheel on the left, so that the mirror wouldn't be of much use to the driver.

The Yonezawa Renault is a much more detailed model. It is shown here in three different colours. *Courtesy of the Bruce Sterling Collection.* Price Category: 6

Side view of the Yonezawa Renault. The wheel designs are very similar to those of the real car.

A very close examination of this photograph will reveal several minor differences between these apparently identical Yonezawa models. *Courtesy of the Bruce Sterling Collection.*

The "1960" number plate presumably gives a clue to the date of the toy. It last appeared in Yonezawa's trade catalogue for 1964, the real Hino-Renault having ceased production in Japan in the previous year.

Although much more stylish, the rear-engined Renault Caravelle can nevertheless trace its ancestry back to the 4CV. This simple but attractive toy is by Ichiko. *Courtesy of the Bruce Sterling Collection.* Price Category: 2

Note the use of plastic for the wheels on the Ichiko Caravelle. *Courtesy of the Bruce Sterling Collection.*

Simca Beaulieu

As it was assembled in Japan by Hino, the Renault 4CV could in one sense be classed as a Japanese car. But there's nothing Japanese about the Simca Beaulieu—except that someone at the Asahi Trading Company thought that it looked a bit like a car built by Toyota, the 1959 Toyopet Crown. As Asahi happened to be making a model of the Crown already, they simply put it in a different box and exported it as a Simca. This was claimed to represent the 1958–61 Simca, a very American looking car, unusual by European standards in having a V8 engine.

Compare the toy with the picture on the box (obviously copied from a contemporary Simca sales brochure) and it has to be admitted that there is a superficial resemblance between these two cars. Both have tailfins and typically 1950s two-tone paintwork. All the same, there's no doubt that the model is a Toyopet and not a Simca—one of the many Toyota cars that Asahi made. The close relationship between the toy company and motor manufacturer was stressed in Asahi's catalogues. "In the close cooperation with Toyota Automobile Company our firm have been releasing excellent model cars one after another in succession. Please available (sic) yourself of this opportunity to stock our durable and beautifully finished model Toys of Toyotas."

The box of this ATC model shows a Simca Vedette Beaulieu but the car inside is a Toyopet Crown. *Courtesy of the Bruce Sterling Collection.* Price Category: 7

This close-up of the front of the Simca/Toyopet shows a considerable amount of complex detailing. *Courtesy of the Bruce Sterling Collection.*

The Simca/Toyopet from the rear. *Courtesy of the Bruce Sterling Collection.*

Although this book concentrates on Japanese models of American and European cars, the Asahi catalogue page reproduced here is a reminder that there was also a vast number of Japanese cars produced too, more for the domestic rather than the export market.

Bandai made the Toyopet Crown as well, to a slightly smaller scale (the model is under nine inches long compared with the 9.5-inch Asahi). In other respects, the Bandai looks very similar to the Asahi, except that Bandai didn't pretend it was a Simca.

Bandai also made the Toyopet Crown. *Courtesy of the Bruce Sterling Collection.*

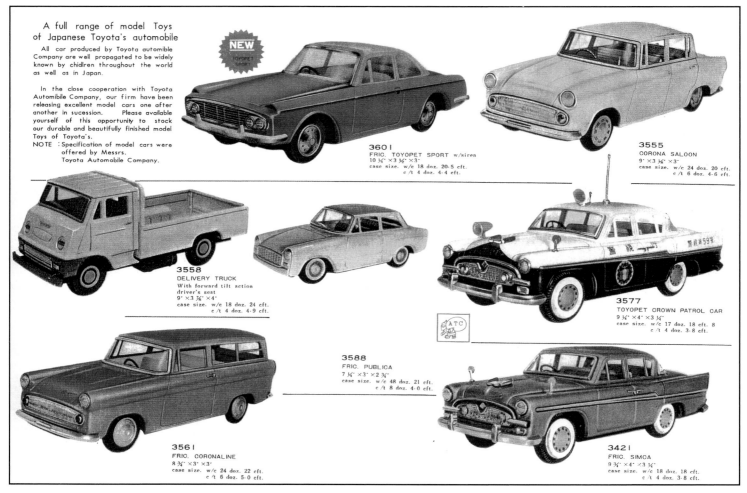

A full range of model Toys of Japanese Toyota's automobile

All car produced by Toyota automobile Company are well propagated to be widely known by chidlren throughout the world as well as in Japan.

In the close cooperation with Toyota Autombile Company, our firm have been releasing excellent model cars one after another in sucession. Please available yourself of this opportunity to stock our durable and beautifully finished model Toys of Toyota's.

NOTE : Specification of model cars were offered by Messrs. Toyota Automobile Company.

3601
FRIC. TOYOPET SPORT w/siren
10 ¼" ×3 ¼" ×3"
case size. w/c 18 doz. 20·5 cft.
c/t 4 doz. 4·9 cft.

3555
CORONA SALOON
9" ×3 ¼" ×3"
case size. w/c 24 doz. 20 cft.
c/t 6 doz. 4·6 cft.

3558
DELIVERY TRUCK
With forward tilt action driver's seat
9" ×3 ¾" ×4"
case size. w/c 18 doz. 24 cft.
c/t 4 doz. 4·9 cft.

3577
TOYOPET CROWN PATROL CAR
9 ¾" ×4" ×3 ¾"
case size. w/c 17 doz. 18 cft. 8
c/t 4 doz. 3·8 cft.

3588
FRIC. PUBLICA
7 ¼" ×3" ×2 ¾"
case size. w/c 48 doz. 21 cft.
c/t 8 doz. 4·0 cft.

3561
FRIC. CORONALINE
8 ¾" ×3" ×3"
case size. w/c 24 doz. 22 cft.
c/t 6 doz. 5·0 cft.

3421
FRIC. SIMCA
9 ¾" ×4" ×3 ¼"
case size. w/c 18 doz. 18 cft.
c/t 4 doz. 3·8 cft.

This page from Asahi's trade catalogue clearly describes the Toyopet as a Simca, and pictures it amongst numerous other Japanese cars. Note the enormous quantities in which wholesalers could order these toys!

German Cars

Volkswagens

No car has been built in greater numbers than the Volkswagen Beetle—not even the Model T Ford. Naturally, this situation is reflected in the model world, too. There are plenty of collectors who specialise entirely in models of the car that Europeans call the "Beetle" and Americans call the "Bug." Books have been published which try to list all the known models and there's a specialist VW Model Club which publishes its own magazine. Even though the real car has been superseded by the new Beetle, new scale models of the original one are still being launched.

It would be impossible to do justice in a few pages to all the Japanese tin Volkswagens ever made, but the four shown here are all interesting in different ways. The smallest, an oval-window Beetle by Masudaya, was available as a construction kit with either electric or clockwork power. The version

Masudaya's battery-operated Volkswagen is operated by an on/off lever on the other side of the car. *Courtesy of the Alex J. Cameron Collection.* Price Category: 2

This Volkswagen convertible by TN has a visible engine, complete with operating pistons. *Courtesy of the Alex J. Cameron Collection.* Price Category: 4

shown here is possibly a later issue, also electrically-operated but with an unorthodox method of accommodating the battery which is inserted vertically rather than horizontally through a flap on the underside of the car. Movement is controlled by a lever on the left hand side of the body.

One of the things that made the Beetle different from other cars was that it had an air-cooled engine mounted at the rear, and Japanese toy makers, always on the lookout for mechanical gimmicks to add to their toys, seized on this feature. The 9.5-inch convertible by TN is one example. The rear engine cover is of clear plastic, allowing a see-through engine to be viewed. When switched on, this lights up and the pistons can be seen operating a rotating crankshaft though the toy itself is powered by a friction motor. Dashboard and door trims are lithographed in tin, but the seats are made of plastic, suggesting that this toy dates from near the end of the tinplate era.

Bandai's larger (16.5-inch) Beetle works on a similar principle but is more elaborate. When the engine is switched on not only do the pistons move but the car emits an engine noise which is a reasonable imitation of the sound of a real Volkswagen motor ticking over. The headlamps as well as the movements of the car itself are electrically operated too, all of this requiring several heavy batteries to make it work. Other moving parts include a sliding sun roof and radio aerial.

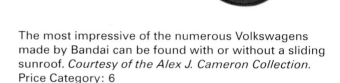

The most impressive of the numerous Volkswagens made by Bandai can be found with or without a sliding sunroof. *Courtesy of the Alex J. Cameron Collection.* Price Category: 6

A close-up of the engine compartment on the Bandai shows a combination of plastic parts and lithographed tin. Not only do the pistons move, but the car emits a Volkswagen-like engine noise. *Courtesy of the Alex J. Cameron Collection.*

The yellow Beetle is ten inches long and comes with a plastic hand control set, allowing forward and reverse movements with a flashing roof light. Neither box nor model gives any clue to the maker, but there is a reference no. 352806. The "ADAC Strassenwacht" markings denote the German equivalent of the British AA (Automobile Association) which offers emergency help to motorists. The model is therefore an example of how Japanese toys were often tailored to the needs of the toy market in one specific country. The Volkswagen Microbus in "Polizei" livery is a similar example. Again, the maker is not identified.

This yellow Beetle in "ADAC Strassenwacht" livery carries no maker's name, but a very similar green and white "Polizei" model exists which has been identified as a Taiyo product. *Courtesy of the Alex J. Cameron Collection.* Price Category: 3

The text on the box makes clear that this toy was specifically produced for the German market. *Courtesy of the Alex J. Cameron Collection.*

This small (6.75-inch) Volkswagen Microbus was also made for sale in Germany. *Courtesy of the Alex J. Cameron Collection.* Price Category: 1

These little VW vans and pickups may not be in the same category as the larger and more detailed tin toys illustrated in the rest of this book, but they are still colourful and attractive items. Numerous different liveries exists, some with cut-out windows and others lithographed with drivers and passengers. The name of the manufacturer is understood to be Endoh. *Courtesy of the Alex J. Cameron Collection.* $15 each.

Sales Office:

TOYOMENKA INC.
ROOM #251 & 253 200 5TH AVE.,
NEW YORK. N.Y.

Bandai CO., LTD.

TOKYO   JAPAN

Bandai
PRINTED IN JAPAN

Opposite page:
This page from the 1969 Bandai trade catalogue shows not only the large Volkswagen model but a smaller version in a box marked "European car series." One can only guess at how much this pile of toys would be worth nowadays .

Messerschmitt, Opel, Mercedes

After the war Messerschmitt could not continue building aircraft and was looking around for other products to occupy its workforce. One of these was a micro car christened the "Kabinenroller" and powered by a two-stroke engine—with steering by handlebars. In 1955 power was increased to 200 cc and it is this model, the KR 200, that Bandai made, along with the German "Bubble Car," the BMW Isetta. The Messerschmitt is an outstanding model, bearing in mind that the very complex curves had to be formed from flat tinplate. Though the glazed canopy has metal window frames these are for decoration rather than reinforcement and this component tends to become scuffed or cracked very easily.

The popularity of such vehicles was short-lived as their drivers soon wanted to move up to "proper" cars as soon as possible. The Opel Kapitan was a 2.5-liter in the upper middle bracket and a good model of it was made by KS. The choice of the Opel would have been understandable as the toy would appeal not only to German buyers but to many

The KS Opel Kapitan features an elaborate "drive all around" system with discs to make the car move in different directions. *Courtesy of the Bruce Sterling Collection.* Price Category: 6

Americans too, as Opels were sold in the States and as many as 1,000,000 had been exported there by 1959. The KS model is eleven inches long and although battery-powered, moves in an unconventional way. Discs are supplied which can be installed in the rear trunk to make the car follow various preset paths.

The rarity of Bandai's Messerschmitt is increased by the fragile plastic canopy which is so easily damaged. *Courtesy of the Bruce Sterling Collection.* Price Category: 7

This view of the Opel shows the colourful box and the various discs required to operate the car. *Courtesy of the Bruce Sterling Collection.*

If the Opel was a somewhat staid family car the Mercedes Benz 300SL was Germany's most glamorous sports car. Its most exotic form is the coupe, whose famous "gullwing" doors were fitted on a tinplate model by Tsukuda and pictured in Kitahara's book *1000 Tin Toys*. Shown here is the hardtop convertible in an eleven-inch version by TN. This has a remote-control mechanism operated by the same hand-held "dashboard" fitted to the Buick shown on page 30.

The TN Mercedes 300SL uses the remote-control system fitted to the same maker's Buick. *Courtesy of the Bruce Sterling Collection.* Price Category: 5

Motorcycles

The main focus of this book is, of course, on cars, but if Bandai considered a model of a Vespa scooter worthy of inclusion in its "Model Auto Series" then surely motorcycles deserve a mention here. There were plenty of Japanese tinplate motorcycles, but most tended to be very toy-like, often with unrealistic riders or large stabilizing wheels. The three pictured here, however, are recognizable models of real machines.

The popularity of the motor scooter started as an Italian phenomenon but it quickly spread to the younger generation in other countries too. Inevitably, numerous small-scale replicas appeared such as the diecast ones by Mercury of Italy and Dalia of Spain. Bandai's 8.5-inch model is considerably bigger, allowing room for the obligatory friction motor to fit underneath the seat.

As a means of transport the Vespa is hardly in the same league as the more powerful machine also modelled by Bandai, the Meguro motorcycle (ref. 568). Meguro was a Japanese motorcycle company which produced English-style bikes between 1937 and 1964, until the firm was eventually absorbed by Kawasaki. The model pictured is somewhat unusual in being completely white instead of the more

Although it is not a car, Bandai's Vespa scooter was part of the "Model Auto Series". *Courtesy of Douglas R. Kelly.* Price Category: 3

common black which had lithographed Meguro markings on the chrome gas tank. To find this twelve-inch long friction model with all its many parts intact is very difficult indeed, and the box is even rarer than the bike itself.

This Meguro motorcycle, also by Bandai, is usually black. The white version is rarer. *Courtesy of the Bruce Sterling Collection.* Price Category: 9

The Meguro motorcycle from the rear. As with most toy motorcycles, stabilising wheels had to be added to keep the model upright. *Courtesy of the Bruce Sterling Collection.*

It is always a problem to keep a two-wheel model upright. Bandai solved this by fitting two small stabilizing wheels, but another solution was to link the cycle to a sidecar—a far more common sight on the roads in the 1950s than today. Marusan took this approach with their model of a 1954 Sunbeam S7, based on a machine made by the respected British firm founded in 1912. Smaller than the Meguro, the Marusan is 9.5 inches long and 5 inches high. The wheels are particularly realistic, having individually cut out spokes, whereas the Bandai had solid discs. The presence of the sidecar has another purpose as well as providing stability; it houses the batteries which power the toy. There is an on/off switch on the sidecar while an additional switch on the bike itself has two speed settings. As always, there are colour variations: sometimes the cycle has a chrome finish or a black or maroon sidecar. The Sunbeam was also available on its own, minus the sidecar and electric motor.

This Marusan motorcycle is based on a British prototype, the Sunbeam. *Courtesy of the Bruce Sterling Collection.* Price Category: 10

Marusan cleverly used the sidecar to house the batteries needed to power the toy. *Courtesy of the Bruce Sterling Collection.*

Side by side: the Bandai Meguro (left) with the Marusan Sunbeam (right). *Courtesy of the Bruce Sterling Collection.*

CHAPTER FOUR

From Tinplate to Diecast

Mercedes Benz 220SE by Cherryca Phenix, one of the most sought-after of all Japanese diecasts. *Courtesy of the Bruce Sterling Collection.* $400+.

A bewildering variety of names and trademarks can be found on diecast toys made in Japan: Asahi, Model Pet, Micro Pet, Diapet, Sakura, Tomica, Cherryca Phenix. . .to name only a few. But who made what? Which ones are actually the same models under different names? This chapter certainly won't provide all the answers, but it will shed at least some light on a complex subject.

Background

While Japanese tin toy cars were still produced in large numbers throughout the 1960s and even into the seventies, smaller-scale diecasts were gradually becoming more popular. The reasons are not difficult to find. Although the tin toys shown in the previous chapters are remarkably accurate likenesses of the real vehicles, it must be remembered that only the very best examples of this type of product have been shown. There were also vast numbers of much cheaper, poor quality friction toy cars. Far greater realism could be achieved in diecast metal without the labour-intensive finishing and assembly processes involved in the production of the high-end tin toys. In western export markets, tinplate was in any case increasingly viewed as an old-fashioned material with sharp edges that made it unsafe for the manufacture of children's playthings. Moreover, as will be shown in Chapter Five of this book, plastic friction cars made in Hong Kong were rapidly encroaching on the market for tin cars.

Changes in the domestic toy market in Japan were an equally important factor. The toy trade between Japan, America, and Europe no longer operated in one direction only. British diecasts like Dinky, Corgi, and Matchbox were now being imported into Japan and local toymakers quickly saw that there was a considerable local demand for such products. The Asahi Toy Company played a key role in this respect, importing Dinky and Corgi into Japan and even setting up a model car collectors' club to encourage the collecting hobby. It was a natural step for Asahi to move from bringing in other companies' diecasts to making its own. Being at once a producer and an importer of similar toys might suggest that Asahi was effectively competing against itself, but the company did not seem to see any contradiction here, and Asahi's contemporary catalogues show pictures of Dinky and Corgi cars alongside its own products.

Japanese toy companies therefore began to take an interest in diecasts, even though it was a long time before they completely superseded their traditional tin toys. Of the major brands, Asahi launched the Model Pet Series in 1959, soon to be followed by the Taiseiya Company who brought out the Micro Pet Series in 1961. An attempt was made to launch a third brand, Miniature Pet, in 1962 but only one model, an Opel Kapitan, was made. Next, Micro Pet was relaunched under a new name, Cherryca Phenix. The Cherryca Phenix moulds were in turn taken over in about 1965 by Yonezawa, who then started a major new 1/43 scale brand called Diapet. Later, another major toy maker—Tomy—jumped on the bandwagon. As the relationship between all these names can be somewhat confusing, it may be simpler to show them in the form of a table:

1959:	Model Pet Series by Asahi (ATC)
1961:	Micro Pet Series by Taiseiya
1962:	Micro Pet adopts Cherryca Phenix name
1962:	Miniature Pet Series by Nakayama Shoten
1965:	Cherryca Phenix taken over by Yonezawa, who launches Diapet
1970:	Small-scale Tomica series by Tomy
1972:	Tomy launches larger (c.1/40) Tomica-Dandy series

The later Diapet issues and the Tomica series are still current and fairly easy to obtain, with full listings being available in books such as Paolo Rampini's *Golden Book of Model Cars.* A complete history of Tomica diecasts is also available in a book by Vic Davey. On the other hand, the early Model Pet, Micro Pet, and Cherryca Phenix ranges are extremely rare and remain something of a mystery to collectors. It is therefore on these three names that this chapter will concentrate, illustrating many models which are rarely seen in the United States, although at least some of the Cherryca Phenixes did find their way to Europe.

There was a small number of even more obscure Japanese diecast brands which briefly produced only a handful of models, and these deserve a mention first.

Earlier Brands: Linemar and Marusan

Japanese diecasts originated in a similar way to the first post-war tin toys, being made for toy distributors in the USA. In 1958 or 1959 six cars were made by Kuramochi, a company whose history stretches back to pre-war days. Not surprisingly, the cars were all based on American vehicles—a Lincoln, Ford, Edsel, Buick, Pontiac and Chevrolet. A further batch consisted of sports cars, all but one being European cars, though still aimed at the American market, where imported sports cars were very popular. These were a Triumph TR3, a Jaguar XK 150, a BMW 507, Mercedes Benz 300SL, Porsche 356 and a Chevrolet Corvette.

This range was sold under the Collectoy name and distributed in the USA by Linemar (Louis Marx). Often the tooling for model cars can be revamped

The 1958 Pontiac from the Collectoy (Linemar) series of American cars. *Courtesy of Ron Smith.* $60–80

in various ways, and Marx later issued some of the open cars with large Disney cartoon figures driving them. These Linemar models cannot really be compared with later diecasts as they are to a much smaller scale—probably around 1/55 to 1/60 in the case of the American cars. In terms of realism, they are poorly proportioned, the Lincoln being little more than a caricature. Their most serious drawback, however, is that many suffer from metal fatigue—a factor which, paradoxically, increases their desirability to the collector as it makes mint examples harder to track down.

The Lincoln Première is the least realistic of the Collectoy models. *Courtesy of Ron Smith.* $50–$70

Superficially, this red model looks much the same as the blue one, but it does in fact represent a 1958 Buick. *Courtesy of Ron Smith.* $60–80

Some Collectoy models had gold trim applied by hand, as in the case of this Edsel. *Courtesy of Ron Smith.* $60–80

Two of the Collectoy European Sports Cars, the Mercedes 300SL (above) and BMW 507 Coupe (bottom). *Courtesy of Ron Smith.* $60–80

Collectoy Ford Delivery Van. An improvement in casting quality is apparent in this item. Note the different box style featuring the Linemar logo. *Courtesy of Douglas R. Kelly.* $60–80

The Ford Delivery Van was the last of the American vehicles to be added to the range; it comes in a different style of box and does not appear to suffer from fatigue. In size and appearance it is reminiscent of the American "Real Toys" Series by Hubley, while its wheels are very much in the Corgi Toy style. Shown here in pale green in 'Materne Bakery' livery, it also exists in yellow ('Lumar Service'), red ('Linemar Toys') and blue ('Keystone Appliance Co.').

If these Linemar diecasts originate from one familiar source of Japanese toys—an order from an American toy distributor—those by Marusan were inspired by another equally characteristic factor in the history of the Far Eastern toy industry: the use of another firm's designs. Marusan issued a group of seven diecasts which are so like the original Dinky Toys that most people would be unable to tell the difference without looking underneath to read the maker's name. The similarity is so close that it is possible that they were made under license using the original Dinky moulds—a view put forward in the 1970s by the Swiss diecast expert Michel Sordet. It was not unknown for Meccano Limited to dispose of redundant tooling in this way: some Dinky models were later made in India and sold under the name "Nicky Toys."

Some of the Marusans were typically English, like the Morris Mail Van, the Observation Coach, and the Daimler Ambulance, but two were ex-French Dinkies, the Panhard articulated truck and the very

Marusan's Austin Service Car, a very similar casting to the Dinky Toy Austin van which came in "Nestles" and other liveries. *Courtesy of Douglas R. Kelly.* $300+

The inscriptions on the base ensure that the Marusan model can easily be distinguished from the Dinky. *Courtesy of Douglas R. Kelly.*

attractive Ford Milk Truck, complete with ten milk churns. There seems to have been only one original design, a Toyota Toyoace pick-up truck.

This Marusan Panhard articulated lorry is based on the French Dinky "Kodak" truck. Unlike the Dinky, the Marusan did not have a tinplate cover on the trailer. *Courtesy of Douglas R. Kelly.* $300+

Not likely to be seen very often on Japanese roads was the Morris Royal Mail Van, no. 8502 in the Marusan series. *Courtesy of Douglas R. Kelly.* $300+

Details of the base of the Mail Van. The "San" trademark was often used by Marusan, on both tinplate and diecast models. *Courtesy of Douglas R. Kelly.*

The Marusan models came individually boxed in picture cartons with an inscription in poor English "First with the dieca models," obviously a misnomer for "diecast." Perhaps because of their similarity to Dinky Toys, the Marusan range is highly prized and a mint boxed example is unlikely to cost less than $300.

Obviously, plenty of other small groups of diecast toys in various sizes were made in Japan during the early 1960s, some of which can be traced to a particular manufacturer and others whose source will remain a matter for conjecture. For example, various small-scale replicas of vintage cars are often found at collectors' fairs and Masudaya—a firm better known for its mechanical robots—made a few cars vaguely based on American prototypes and issued with a chrome plated finish (hence the "Silver Pet" series). Of course, there were innumerable other items that

A small scale Double Deck Bus, one of many "Matchbox-lookalikes" made in Japan. The box is marked "an Elvin Product." *Courtesy of Douglas R. Kelly.* $15

were sold for a while and then faded away, leaving little clue to their provenance. One such model is the green double-deck bus, one of many small scale toys that were inspired by, and sometimes directly copied from, the Lesney Matchbox series. This one is packed in a blue box simply marked "an Elvin product."

These two items, each less than two inches long, are part of a set of twelve marked "TM." Some of the small diecasts—like the Daimler Ambulance—are influenced by Matchbox products, but the vintage car is not. $8–10

Asahi's Model Pet series

In spite of all these more or less obscure precursors, it was not until October 1959 that a Japanese manufacturer launched anything comparable to European brands such as Solido, Dinky or Corgi—Asahi's "Model Pet" series. The first model in the range was a Toyota Crown Sedan—clearly a significant choice as it indicated that the primary market envisaged was not, as so often before, America, but Japan itself.

Over the next fourteen years more than 50 other cars, plus a few motorcycles, appeared in the Model Pet lineup, every one of them based on a prototype built in Japan. This was something new in the world of diecasts, as no one else had marketed a range of Japanese cars before. Toyotas were the clear favourite, and whenever a new generation of the Crown and Corona was launched, Model Pet would bring out a scale model. A close working relationship between the Asahi Company and Toyota Motors was already in existence and had previously resulted in numerous tinplate Toyotas being made.

A checklist of Model Pet cars can be found on page 154. It contains many names that are still around today, like Nissan, Honda, and Mazda, together with some that are less familiar like the Isuzu Bellet, Hino Contessa, and Prince Skyline. The presence of two typically British family cars, the Hillman Minx and Austin Cambridge, is of course explained by the fact that these were assembled in Japan under license.

At first, there were up to ten new castings per year, but new model announcements slowed down after 1965 and ceased for a time in 1967. More new models arrived in the early seventies but these were noticeably less realistic, particularly regarding the wheel designs. The last introduction was a Nissan Cedric saloon in 1973, with the Asahi company going out of business in 1979.

The Best of the Model Pet Range

In common with most other ranges of model cars, the Model Pet line-up contains a fair number of run-of-the-mill family cars with a sprinkling of more inspired choices; these, of course, are the ones that collectors want.

Model Pet no. 27, a Toyota Corona. Certain items in the Model Pet series were first given a plated finish and then overpainted, allowing "chrome" trim to show through. This process was more extensively employed by Cherryca Phenix. *Courtesy of Douglas R. Kelly.* $100

No. 27, the Toyota Corona, is typical of the former category, an ordinary saloon whose generic styling has little to distinguish it from its European counterparts. A colourful livery can make even a plain saloon car look interesting, as the Nissan Cedric taxi demonstrates very clearly. The fragility of the blue decal strip makes this model particu-larly hard to find in mint condition. To Westerners, that Japanese writing on the side just makes it seem more exotic—even though it probably means nothing more than the charge per mile! In a similar way, the Toyota Crown was dressed up as a black and white police patrol car (no. 12).

Model Pet no. 10, Nissan Cedric Taxi. The fragility of the side decal on this taxi makes it very difficult to find an example in perfect condition. *Courtesy of the Bruce Sterling Collection.* $160–200

Model Pet no. 12SP, Toyota Crown Police Car. The black and white livery of the real car pictured on the box has been accurately rendered on the model. *Courtesy of the Alex J. Cameron Collection.* $160–200.

The two smallest Model Pet cars are popular with collectors, no doubt because of their "cute" shape which gives them an individuality lacking in most of the other saloon cars. Most sought-after is no. 3, the Subaru 360, which was in fact the first car to carry that name, dating from 1958. Comparable to the Fiat 500 in size, the little 360 had its engine at the back, driving the rear wheels. It was for sale (briefly) on the American market but did not catch on.

Model Pet no. 3, Subaru 360. One of the most desirable of the early Model Pets, the Subaru is described as being in 1/36 scale, larger than the rest of the series. *Courtesy of the Bruce Sterling Collection.* $200+

Model Pet no. 3, Subaru 360 in yellow, the most difficult colour to find. *Courtesy of the Bruce Sterling Collection.* $300+

Model Pet no. 3, Subaru 360 in three different colours. In each case the roof panel is painted in a contrasting shade. *Courtesy of the Bruce Sterling Collection.*

In scale terms, the Model Pet version looks quite large, as it is nearer 1/36 scale than 1/42. It is a fine casting, with bumpers picked out in black and a roof panel in a colour contrasting with the bodywork. Among the colours available were blue, green, pink, lilac, cream and—rarest of all—yellow.

Model Pet no. 13 was another attractive small Japanese rear-engined car, the Mazda 360, the first production car from a firm which had been making motorcycles since 1923. The reason that Mazda and Subaru made little cars with engines under 360 cc was simply to do with the tax advantages of this category of vehicle.

Model Pet no. 13, Mazda 360. Made to the more usual 1/42 scale, the Mazda looks tiny compared to the Subaru. *Courtesy of Douglas R. Kelly.* $120

Model Pet no. 13, Mazda 360 in the rare aqua green shade. *Courtesy of the Bruce Sterling Collection.* $200+

Model Pet no. 13, Mazda 360, in gray (left) and aqua green (right). *Courtesy of the Bruce Sterling Collection.*

As it was added to the Model Pet range later than the Subaru, the Mazda has interior fittings as well as window glazing. Usually dark red or white, the aqua green shade is considerably harder to find.

The Model Pet versions of the two British cars assembled in Japan—the Austin Cambridge and the Hillman Minx—are also worth seeking out. These are not only more detailed than home-grown Dinky or Corgi versions but are finished in more attractive two-tone shades as well. The Hillman (pictured here in blue and light green) also came in red, all three having the roof and boot area painted light gray. Note the different wheel centres on the two versions, the model with the white rims being fitted with suspension. The Minx turns up fairly regularly; the Cambridge, on the other hand, is much rarer.

Model Pet no. 9, Hillman Minx, one of the easier to find of the Model Pet series. *Courtesy of the Bruce Sterling Collection.* $130

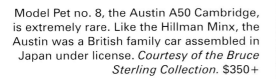

Model Pet no. 9, Hillman Minx. The green/gray Minx is fitted with spring suspension and has different wheel trims from the blue/gray version. *Courtesy of the Bruce Sterling Collection.*

Model Pet no. 8, the Austin A50 Cambridge, is extremely rare. Like the Hillman Minx, the Austin was a British family car assembled in Japan under license. *Courtesy of the Bruce Sterling Collection.* $350+

Micro Pet and Cherryca Phenix

Model Pets can claim to be the first extensive range of diecasts made in Japan, but they did not have the field to themselves for long. Around 1961 the Taiseiya Toy Company launched the Micro Pet series and, as an attempt to offer something different from the competition, fitted the cars with flywheel friction motors—rather like Corgi Toys did in the early days of their rivalry with the long-established Dinky range. Nevertheless, it did seem that Micro Pet was aimed at the same Japanese domestic market as Model Pet, with popular Japanese cars like the Subaru and Mazda 360, Datsun Bluebird, and Hillman Minx appearing in both diecast ranges. Even the similarity of the names Micro Pet and Model Pet might seem to suggest a certain lack of originality.

Micro Pet no. 1, Subaru 360. Like its Model Pet counterpart, the Micro Pet Subaru is to a larger scale than the rest of the series. This time a flywheel friction motor is fitted and the roof panel is not separately painted. *Courtesy of the Bruce Sterling Collection.* $350+

Micro Pet no. 5, Nissan Cedric. The lilac paint may not be to everyone's taste! *Courtesy of the Bruce Sterling Collection.* $200+

These reasons may explain why Micro Pet got off to a rather slow start. The Taiseiya company was quick to revamp the range and after little more than a dozen separate castings had been issued, another brand name was adopted in 1962—Cherryca Phenix, although the Micro Pet name was not completely dropped. Under the new name Taiseiya went on to produce some of the most original and attractive diecast toys ever made and these now command the very highest prices from discerning collectors.

Micro Pet no. 14, Prince Microbus. The top and bottom sections on this model are both red, but "three-tone" colour schemes exist too. There was also a "gold"-plated version of this and certain other Model Pets (see Appendix I for details). *Courtesy of the Bruce Sterling Collection.* $300+

The plated version of the Prince Microbus. *Courtesy of the Bruce Sterling Collection.* $300+

Micro Pet no. 17 Datsun Light Van, in effect a station wagon version of the Datsun Bluebird saloon. *Courtesy of the Bruce Sterling Collection.* $250+

Micro Pet no. 11, the Prince Skyway Estate. The vehicle is not unlike the Datsun, but it comes in more striking two-tone colours. It has also been seen in yellow/red. *Courtesy of the Bruce Sterling Collection.* $250+

The styling of the Prince Skyway shows more American influence compared to the more restrained Datsun. *Courtesy of the Bruce Sterling Collection.*

A group of four Micro Pet models. Back row: no. 17 Ford Falcon Police Car, no. 14 Prince Microbus, no. 9 Chevrolet Impala; front: no. 1 Subaru 360. All of these have friction motors. *Courtesy of the Bruce Sterling Collection.*

The direction in which Cherryca Phenix was to develop had already been anticipated in the Micro Pet range with the inclusion of two American cars, a Chevrolet Impala and Ford Falcon, both of which were carried over into the new Cherryca Phenix range. Not only were further American cars modeled, but European ones too, and the range was in fact exported to Europe.

One thing that sets these cars apart from others is that the raw material used to make the castings contained a substance called antimony, a brittle silvery-white semi-metallic chemical element. One of the properties of antimony is that it expands on solidifying and this makes it a very useful ingredient of alloys used for casting as the expansion of the alloy helps to force the material into the mould, enabling finer detailing to be cast into the toy. Another novel feature was that the the window frames, bumpers, and grilles were masked during painting, allowing the bare metal to show through on the finished product to give the effect of a chrome finish.

All this is fascinating to the specialist collector now, but the Cherryca Phenix range did not make a great impact at the time. For one thing, it seems that the toys did not do very well in export markets. It is surely significant that of the first 23 Cherryca Phenix models, seven were European cars and seven American, while the remaining 27 items were Japanese cars (with one exception, and that was a different version of the Mercedes Benz 300SL already in the range). It would appear, then, that after an attempt to break into the European market, Cherryca Phenix decided to concentrate on Japan.

Yet the Cherryca Phenix series was not especially successful at home either. One reason could have been that the different alloy used made these cars less robust in the hands of children. It's said that some unscrupulous toy representatives, anxious to increase their commission, used to visit small toy shops, buy a Cherryca Phenix and crush it in the presence of the shopkeeper in an attempt to prove that these were inferior to other toy cars!

After little more than three years, Cherryca Phenix ceased production. In 1965 Taiseiya was absorbed by Yonezawa, which is today part of the still larger Sega Company. Some of the Cherryca models ended up as part of Yonezawa's Diapet range.

The Best of the Cherryca Phenix Range

Cherryca Phenix sales may have been modest at the time but today collectors will pay huge sums for these toys. The range conveniently divides into three categories: American, European and Japanese cars. The remainder of this chapter will illustrate some fine examples of these scarce models.

American Cars

The remarkable thing about the American cars is that they are so appealing even when they are not very accurate—some being rather poorly proportioned and most having oversized wheels.

One of the more accurately shaped models is the Chevrolet Impala, which at first sight has a familiar look about it, possibly because of its similarity to the much commoner Corgi Toy. The Impala

illustrates how some of the earlier Micro Pets
evolved into Cherryca Phenixes. It first appeared as
Micro Pet no. F-9 in two-tone colours, and F-10 as a
black and white police car with paper stickers on
the doors (on which, unfortunately, the glue invariably seeps through, causing surface discolouration
even on the most pristine examples). The first version of the car had a friction mechanism—the flywheel is visible through the back window—but by
the time it re-emerged as no. 5 in the Cherryca
Phenix series it had acquired plastic interior fittings
instead.

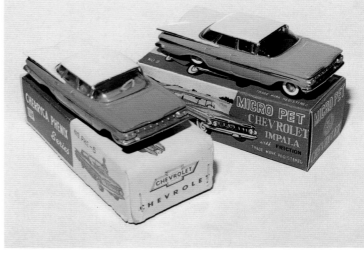

Apart from the box styles, the main difference between the
Cherryca Phenix Impala (left) and the earlier Micro Pet (right)
is that the former has interior fittings while the latter has a
friction motor. *Courtesy of the Bruce Sterling Collection.*
Micro Pet, $400+; Cherryca Phenix, $300.

Underneath, the two Impalas are easily distin-
guished by their different baseplates. The
Cherryca Phenix (left) is painted gray while the
Micro Pet (right) is black. *Courtesy of the Bruce
Sterling Collection.*

Front view of the Cherryca Phenix no.
5, Chevrolet Impala (left) and Micro
Pet (right). *Courtesy of the Bruce
Sterling Collection.*

Apart from the entirely different box styles for the two models, note the variations in baseplate design. The Micro Pet's is black and incorporates the "two children" logo, while the Cherryca's is gray.

One other American car can be found in both these ranges, the 1960 Ford Falcon (originally Micro Pet no. F-12) which came in numerous tasteful duotone colours. Apart from the two-tone green, white/pale blue, and metallic green/white shown here, red/black, orange/black, and maroon/white have been recorded. There was even a gold-plated version, too. No. F-13 was a police car in a livery identical to that of the Chevrolet.

The rare Micro Pet Ford Falcon police car ($400+) with three different colour variations on the Cherryca Phenix issue and two different Micro Pets. *Courtesy of the Bruce Sterling Collection.*

Micro Pet no. 12, Ford Falcon in metallic blue and cream. *Courtesy of the Bruce Sterling Collection.* $400

Micro Pet no. 12, Ford Falcon, in red and black. This may be a very early issue as it has different wheels from the other Falcons. *Courtesy of the Bruce Sterling Collection.* $400

Close-up of the rear of the Micro Pet Falcon, with the flywheel friction mechanism visible through the back window. *Courtesy of the Bruce Sterling Collection.*

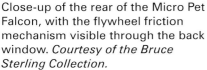

One further variation on the Falcon can be found, the "Flasher Lamp" car with electric front, rear and interior lighting, and a battery compartment underneath. The only other car to receive this treatment was a 1960 Buick Electra and the photograph opposite clearly shows the difference between this version and the regular Cherryca Phenix one. The tinplate base has a hinged cover to allow access to the battery and an on/off switch on the side of the car. Apart from having plastic lenses for the lights, the two models are identical.

Micro Pet Flasher Lamp Series no. 1 was a variation of the Cherryca Phenix Buick Electra no. 6. The battery was inserted in the compartment underneath and the lights were controlled by the switch behind the front wheel. *Courtesy of the Bruce Sterling Collection.* $350

Cherryca Phenix no. 6, Buick Electra, in two different colour schemes ($300 each), with the Flasher Lamp model in gray. *Courtesy of the Bruce Sterling Collection.*

Four more American cars belong to the Cherryca Phenix lineup. No. 17, the Lincoln Continental, is the easiest to find and it is shown here in three two-tone colour schemes. The model is not unlike the more familiar one by Tekno of Denmark, although it looks rather small compared to the Tekno, being approximately 1/50 scale.

Cherryca Phenix no. 17, the Lincoln Continental, seems to be easier to find that the rest of the series. *Courtesy of the Bruce Sterling Collection.* $275

Two colour schemes on the Lincoln. *Courtesy of the Bruce Sterling Collection.*

Like the Lincoln, the 1962 Ford Thunderbird hard top is not well-proportioned but it is still a desirable model. Cherryca's chrome-plating method is used to good effect here, showing through the paint to produce a chrome strip along the top edge of the bodywork.

Cherryca Phenix no. 15, the Ford Thunderbird, not the best proportioned of the series. *Courtesy of the Bruce Sterling Collection.* $300

The 1961 Dodge Polara, with its unusual reversed rear fins, was overlooked at the time by model car companies, though the British Lone Star firm included a similar Dodge Dart coupe in their Roadmaster series. Again, the style of the real car allowed Cherryca Phenix plenty of scope for chrome detailing.

The final American car was no. 20, a 1962 Cadillac. If the proportions are somewhat suspect because of the large wheels, this flaw is balanced to an extent by the delicacy of the slim window pillars. This is the hardest to find of the American cars, with the silvery-blue metallic one being especially rare.

Cherryca Phenix no. 10, the Dodge Polara. The similarity between the wheel styles and those of Danish Tekno models has often been noted. *Courtesy of the Bruce Sterling Collection.* $300

Cherryca Phenix no. 20, the Cadillac, is the last and hardest to find of the 1960s American cars. The metallic blue is extremely rare. *Courtesy of the Bruce Sterling Collection.* Black, $350+. Metallic blue, $500+.

Cherryca Phenix no. 20, Cadillac in black. Note the different wheel styles compared to the Dodge Polara. *Courtesy of the Bruce Sterling Collection.* $350+

European Cars

Cherryca Phenix only modelled a handful of European cars—but they showed exceptionally good judgment in the ones they picked and some of these could convincingly claim to be the finest replicas of the prototype that were made at the time. The group comprised two Mercedes, two Volkswagens, a Citroen and a Jaguar. Of these, the Jaguar is probably the least successful, with its slightly clumsy opening hood.

The Mercedes 300SL first appeared as an open sports (PHE 3) and then with a removable hardtop (PHE 11) made of metal without a cut-out rear window. Later on, when increasing competition in the diecast market dictated the fitting of opening parts, a redesigned 300SL was made (PHE 29) with a separate and rather heavy front grille/bumper component.

Cherryca Phenix no. 11, Mercedes-Benz 300SL Hardtop. Unlike most models of this type, the removable roof section is made of metal rather than plastic. *Courtesy of the Bruce Sterling Collection.* $350+

Cherryca Phenix no. 29 was a completely different version of the Mercedes 300SL, a later issue with opening parts and packed in the newer style of box. The entire front section is one heavy chrome-plated part. *Courtesy of the Bruce Sterling Collection.* $350+

Cherryca Phenix no. 29 (left) and no. 11 (right) placed side by side for comparison. *Courtesy of the Bruce Sterling Collection.*

The Citroen and the Volkswagen Karmann Ghia, on the other hand, are as near to diecast perfection as any collector could hope for. The Cherryca Phenix Citroen convertible—based on a prototype designed and built by French coachbuilders Henri Chapron—is a heavy, impressive item with an interior made of metal rather than the more usual plastic. The windscreen is exactly right, unlike the earlier French model by JRD which suffers from an oversize screen, but this is inevitably the toy's most fragile feature. Rarely to be found on the open market, a Cherryca Phenix Citroen could easily go for $600 in mint and boxed condition.

Cherryca Phenix no. 19, Citroen DS19 Convertible. Highly sought-after, particularly among French collectors. The perspex windscreen is easily broken. *Courtesy of the Bruce Sterling Collection.* $400+

Cherryca Phenix no. 19, Citroen DS 19 Convertible in two different colours. *Courtesy of the Bruce Sterling Collection.* $400+

Note the different steering wheels on the two Citroens, although neither resembles that of the real car, which had only one spoke. *Courtesy of the Bruce Sterling Collection.*

Chapron modified the Citroen saloon into convertibles and coupes, but Karmann of Osnabrück in Germany went much further with the Volkswagen Beetle chassis, creating an entirely different car to a design by Ghia of Italy: the Volkswagen Karmann Ghia. The coupe went into production in 1955 with a convertible being offered two years later. Models of the coupe can be found in various mainstream diecast ranges such as Dinky Toys and Märklin but the convertible was less frequently chosen. Unusually, Cherryca Phenix fitted not only a windscreen but side windows too. Note the wheel variations on the particular examples shown here; the white inner rims are reminiscent of the style used by Tekno of Denmark.

Cherryca Phenix no. 9, Volkswagen Karmann Ghia convertible, one of the very few models made of this vehicle in open-top form. *Courtesy of the Bruce Sterling Collection.* $400+

Interior details of the Karmann Ghia. The steering wheel is of the same design as the one fitted to the gray Citroen. *Courtesy of the Bruce Sterling Collection.*

Three colour schemes on the Karmann Ghia. *Courtesy of the Bruce Sterling Collection.*

Less glamorous, perhaps, but just as desirable in model form, is the VW Beetle itself. The box describes this as an "Export Beetle." Turn indicator lights were first mounted on the top of the front wings on American-market Volkswagens in 1958, eventually becoming standard on other Beetles in 1961, and this feature is present on the Cherryca model. The car is shown here in dark blue and in green; it can also be found in red.

Cherryca Phenix no. 8, an accurate replica of the Volkswagen Beetle. *Courtesy of the Bruce Sterling Collection.* $400+

Cherryca Phenix no. 8, the Volkswagen in dark blue. *Courtesy of the Bruce Sterling Collection.* $400+

Front and rear details of the Volkswagen. *Courtesy of the Bruce Sterling Collection.*

The Mercedes Benz 220 SE was a dignified car with plenty of chrome trim, and the Cherryca Phenix captures its "formal" look rather well, even though the characteristic three-pointed star radiator mascot is not represented. A close examination of the black and cream cars photographed will again show minor variations in the wheel patterns used. The Mercedes also exists in metallic blue, green, and red.

Cherryca Phenix no. 18, Mercedes-Benz 220SE. The model, like the real car, is characterised by lavish amounts of "chrome." *Courtesy of the Bruce Sterling Collection.* $350+

The Mercedes looks equally good in cream or in black. *Courtesy of the Bruce Sterling Collection.* $350 each.

This red Mercedes-Benz is particularly scarce. *Courtesy of the Bruce Sterling Collection.* $400+

However one attempts to subdivide a range of models, there will always be some that defy classification. There's one other item that can be included here, as it's European, but it isn't a car at all: the Fordson Major Tractor. If it looks familiar, this is because it seems to be a copy of the Corgi Toy model which had come out in 1961. Even the steering link mechanism is the same. Complete with a trailer carrying four milk churns, this is a very "English"-looking toy, quite different in style from the cars in the range—but every bit as desirable.

The Cherryca Phenix Fordson Major Tractor is rather different from the rest of the series. It comes complete with four milk churns in the trailer. *Courtesy of the Bruce Sterling Collection.* $300–400

Japanese Cars

The rest of the Cherryca Phenix range consisted of Japanese cars for the home market. Today, of course, Japanese cars can be seen all over American and European roads, but in the 1960s they were much less familiar outside their country of origin. Inevitably, then, this group of Cherryca Phenixes appeals mostly to Japanese collectors.

It was a happy coincidence that Cherryca started to make models of Japanese cars when they did, for this was the time when indigenous car makers were gradually leaving behind their links with European companies and developing their own original designs. The Hino Contessa, no. 1 in the Cherryca range, is a case in point. The car was developed out of the Renault 4CV, which Hino assembled under license; it also resembles the later Renault Dauphine, yet it is very much Hino's own design. Similarly, no. 13, the Nissan/Datsun 1200 pickup, was a vehicle devised for local needs. It's by no means the only pick-up truck to be developed from a saloon car but few retain the rear seating area as this one does. In contrast, no. 14, the Isuzu Bellel, looks very much like a conventional European 'three-box' design with the two-tone paintwork fashionable at the time.

Cherryca Phenix no. 1, Hino Contessa, a car which retained some of the features of the Renaults previously assembled by Hino under license. *Courtesy of the Bruce Sterling Collection.* $250–300

Cherryca Phenix no. 13, Datsun 1200 Pickup, an unusual body style with an extended cabin. *Courtesy of the Bruce Sterling Collection.* $250-$300

Cherryca Phenix no. 14, Isuzu Bellel De Luxe. *Courtesy of the Bruce Sterling Collection.* $250–350

Anyone who likes the MGB and Austin Healey Sprite will immediately be taken with the Datsun Fairlady—a name which the Nissan company still uses for its sports models and which apparently was first adopted in 1960 because Nissan's president had enjoyed seeing 'My Fair Lady' on Broadway. As always with model sports cars of this type, the fragility of the perspex windshield makes perfect examples hard to come by.

Cherryca Phenix no. 16, Datsun Fairlady. Like the other convertibles, the Datsun has a very fragile windshield. *Courtesy of the Bruce Sterling Collection.* $300–350

Everyone has heard of Nissan, but the Prince Motor Company is not nearly as widely known outside Japan. Its origins lie in the Tachikawa Aircraft Company and the Prince name was adopted in 1955 in honour of Crown Prince Hirohito. The Prince Gloria (no. 24) is a big, ponderous-looking six-cylinder saloon produced between 1961 and 1966, the year that Prince merged with Nissan. Thereafter Prince cars were sold as Nissans, even though Nissan was building similar models of its own, such

as the Cedric, the company's first big post-war luxury car. The Cherryca model of the Cedric has the front end treatment and horizontal twin headlamps fitted to the car from 1962 onwards. By this stage, operating features like an opening bonnet were being fitted to Cherryca Phenix models to keep up with the competition. This feature can be seen on the third large Japanese car in the series, the Toyopet (Toyota) Crown, shown here in taxi livery; it also came as a police car.

Cherryca Phenix no. 24, Prince Gloria, a Japanese car from the luxury end of the market. *Courtesy of the Bruce Sterling Collection.* $250–300

Cherryca Phenix no. 25, Nissan Cedric. This is a later, longer-wheelbase version of the Cedric than the one made by Model Pet. By now opening parts were starting to appear on Cherryca Phenix models. *Courtesy of the Bruce Sterling Collection.* $250–300

Cherryca Phenix no. 37, Toyopet Crown Taxi, another very rare variation, especially sought-after in Japan. *Courtesy of the Bruce Sterling Collection.* $500+

Towards the end of production—around 1964-65—Cherryca Phenix experimented with a new and unorthodox box style. The upper and lower sections are in orange cardboard with the ends angled inwards and a separate "wrapper" holding them together—rather like a box of chocolates! Fortunately, the models inside were much more impressive, and the two coupes shown here—a Toyota Corona Coupe and a Prince Sprint—are particularly stylish.

Cherryca Phenix no. 40, Toyota
Corona Sport. Note the redesigned
box style, from which the sliding
wrapper can often be missing.
*Courtesy of the Bruce Sterling
Collection.* $300

Cherryca Phenix no. 39,
Prince Sprint. *Courtesy of
the Bruce Sterling Collection.* $300

Cherryca Phenix no. 30, Isuzu
Bellet. Models of Japanese
vehicles such as this are far more
sought after in Japan than in
either the United States or
Europe. *Courtesy of the Bruce
Sterling Collection.* $300

Yonezawa Takes Over

When Yonezawa bought over the Cherryca Phenix moulds the new owners carried over some of the models into a new diecast range: Diapet. The catalogue page reproduced on page 158 dates from 1969 and reveals that various Cherryca models—such as the Mercedes—were modified and continued into the new series. The Diapet range was still around in the 1990s by which time it had grown to a very extensive one indeed. It included a few European cars—such as another VW Beetle and a Porsche—but the emphasis was mostly on Japanese vehicles. The general "feel" of a later Diapet model, however, is comparable to any other diecast of the time: the individuality of the Cherryca Phenix series has gone.

Miniature Pet

By now, the difference between Model Pet and Micro Pet should be clear—but to make things even more difficult, there was a third make called Miniature Pet as well. According to the Japanese toy expert Noboru Nakajima, this range appeared in 1962 and the maker was Nakayama Shoten. 'Range' is hardly the right word, however, as only one model was ever produced—an Opel Kapitan. This appears to represent the 1958 model, though the box picture is more like its rebodied 1959 successor. The car looks very much like a European diecast but is unusual in having a lithographed tin interior. Underneath it carries the description "Miniature Pet no. 1 Opel Germany" and a logo based on the letter "N" against an elliptical background. Sadly, the model did not catch on; perhaps the Opel was too obscure a choice for Japanese buyers, or perhaps it failed to break into the market because Model Pet and Micro Pet were already too well-established.

Collectors have often wondered why all these ranges contain the name 'Pet'. According to Japanese collectors, this seems to mean nothing more than "small" or "cute"—which is no doubt what diecast cars would seem to be compared to the large tinplate cars that were previously the norm in Japan. Apparently, Toyota's small passenger car, the SA of 1947, was always known by the nickname "Toyopet" and model cars were referred to in similar terms.

Miniature Pet no. 1, the Opel Kapitan, the only item in this series. Available in metallic blue or brown. *Courtesy of the Bruce Sterling Collection.* $500

Postscript: The Sakura "World Famous Cars" series

The subsequent history of Japanese diecasts in the 1970s and 1980s, dominated by Tomica and Diapet, is too vast a subject to tackle here. However, it is fitting to end this chapter by fast-forwarding the story to the early eighties with a brief look at just one group of five models as in a way they marked a return to the distinctive style of the original Cherryca Phenix cars.

Diapet D-138 Toyopet Corona Hardtop. After buying over the Cherryca Phenix moulds the much larger Yonezawa Toy Company went on to produce the extensive Diapet range, still in production in the 1990s. Although more conventional features like plastic interior fittings were adopted, some of the earlier models continued to use the Cherryca Phenix method of representing chrome trim. *Courtesy of Douglas R. Kelly.* $50–60

Tomica Dandy F14, Citroen H Van "Michelin." Diapet and Tomica were the big names in Japanese diecast in the seventies. As with previous Japanese ranges, Tomica modelled numerous European vehicles, such as this Citroen van, which came in several different liveries. *Courtesy of Douglas R. Kelly.* $30

In about 1975 a Mr. Kojima produced a small series of white metal models in Japan under the Rubicon name, one of which was this Renault 4CV. These models are already difficult to find. *Courtesy of the Bruce Sterling Collection.* $100+

The maker is Sakura, and the five cars in question belong to the "World Famous Car Series." The series consisted of a Rolls Royce, Cadillac, Jaguar E Type, Mercedes 220SE and VW Beetle—all of them having reached classic car status by the time that Sakura modelled them.

These cars come in luxurious flock-covered red boxes with the model inside wrapped in a cloth. The toys themselves must be among the heaviest ever made and have the feel of a white metal rather than a diecast model. So heavy are they, in fact, that their suspension is barely strong enough to support the axles. The five make an impressive line-up, standing out from others by virtue of their gleaming chrome achieved by a revival of the

This Rolls Royce is no. A-1 in the Sakura "World Famous Car Series." The method of construction harks back to the earlier Cherryca Phenix series. *Courtesy of the Bruce Sterling Collection.* $40

Sakura A-2, Mercedes Benz 220SE, a car that was also modelled by Cherryca Phenix in a smaller scale. *Courtesy of the Bruce Sterling Collection.* $40

earlier Cherryca Phenix method of plating the whole car prior to painting.

Cadillac expert Jeffrey C. Gurski remarks that the Sakura Cadillac has a "strange visual likeness to a scaled-down Japanese tin toy." That's a significant comment; with the World Famous Car Series, Japanese toymakers could be said to have returned to their roots. The development of the Japanese diecast had come full circle.

Sakura A-3, the Cadillac Fleetwood, the most original of the series—and the most sought-after. *Courtesy of the Bruce Sterling Collection.* $70

Sakura A-4, Jaguar E Type, is perhaps the least successful of the five "World Famous Cars." *Courtesy of the Bruce Sterling Collection.* $40

Sakura A-5, Volkswagen, is incorrectly marked "Volks Wargen" underneath. This model also came in a bright lemon shade. $60

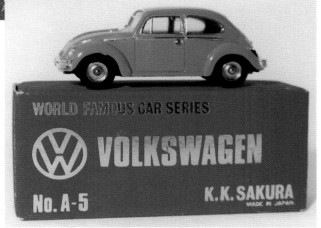

CHAPTER FIVE

The Hong Kong Toy Industry, 1948–1970

A Mercedes Benz 220SE from the Clifford Series—a typical example of the hundreds of different Hong Kong-made plastic friction drive cars from the 1960s, many of which were copied from Dinky, Corgi, or Matchbox diecasts. $30

It is not uncommon for a child to take good care of an expensive toy and even to cherish it into adult life—but who would bother to hang onto a cheap plastic plaything made in Hong Kong? However, it is often the most ephemeral products, thrown away by one generation, that become desired collectors' items to the next. Long despised by collectors as inferior to tinplate or diecast models, plastic friction cars from Hong Kong are now coming into their own. Increasing numbers of variations are being discovered, all of which only adds to the fascination of collecting them. However, with the exception of occasional references in collecting journals there is no literature on the subject available and even less is known about the history of the Hong Kong toy industry than its Japanese counterpart. The aim of this chapter is therefore to sketch the economic background to the development of the Hong Kong toy industry and to explain something about the distribution system that led to its products being exported in huge quantities. The next chapter will then go on to present a selection of the toys themselves.

Economic Background

In British hands from 1843 until 1997, Hong Kong originally prospered as a result of its favoured position as the centre of a flourishing trade between Europe and the Far East. But its economy developed in a completely different direction after World War II, when Hong Kong became more industrialized, finding a ready market in Southeast Asia for consumer goods which were in such short supply at the time. Economic development accelerated after 1949 when the Communist takeover of China caused refugees to flood into Hong Kong. Most were virtually destitute, but some were wealthy businessmen, the former providing a ready source of manpower while the latter brought with them capital and technological expertise. Of course, Hong Kong still derived many benefits from being under British administration. The colony enjoyed access to the British market on preferential terms and when America placed restrictions on products originating from the People's Republic of China in 1952, Hong Kong was well placed to take advantage of the situation.

All these factors, then, led to the rapid expansion of industries such as textiles, plastics, fancy goods, and toys. Plastic manufacture in Hong Kong commenced around 1948. By 1959 there were over 300 plastics factories in Hong Kong, and only six years later that total had risen to 1200. Many of these specialised in toy production; Great Britain not only supplied much of the raw material but received back the finished products in the form of toy exports. In 1958, for example, 25% of Hong Kong's £4 million worth of toy exports went to Britain.[1]

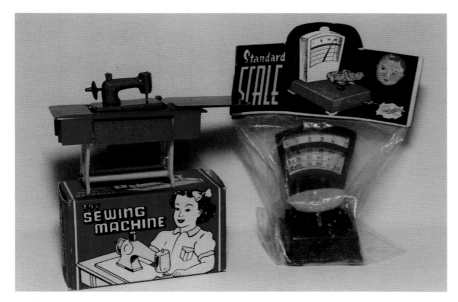

Simple, easily broken toys such as these were churned out in huge quantities in Hong Kong and sold very cheaply. The header card for the scales carries the name of the distributor, Telsalda, who later specialised in friction-drive cars. $8

In the 1970s rising oil prices led to an increase in the cost of plastics as these are, of course, byproducts of the petrochemicals industry. The growth of other low-cost economies in Asia also tended to make Hong Kong's traditional fancy goods and toys less competitive. Once again, though, Hong Kong showed its adaptability by quickly turning to other types of products, particularly electron-

ics, which in the mid-1970s overtook plastics as an export commodity.

But this did not mean the end of the Hong Kong toy industry, which remained as adaptable as ever to changing conditions. In 1978 China became open to foreign investment, and special economic development zones were set up. Not for the first time in the colony's history, a low-cost Chinese labour force became available. This time, instead of refugees coming into Hong Kong, it was the manufacturers who relocated their factories over the border in Guangdong province on the Chinese mainland, which rapidly industrialised as a result of Hong Kong capital. Today there is hardly any toy production in Hong Kong itself, the pattern being for toy companies to have their head offices in Hong Kong with manufacturing facilities in Guangdong.

Distribution System

Some of the most successful of these companies, such as Maisto and Yat Ming, now distribute their products worldwide under their own trademarks and have offices in many different countries. But in the early days of toy manufacture in Hong Kong things were done much more casually. Hong Kong's historical ties with Great Britain meant that it was natural that many of the colony's products would find their way to the British Isles. Numerous long-established trading companies had been bringing goods in from the Far East since the nineteenth century and toys started to be imported through the same channels. One such company was Graham Brothers of 73 Endell Street, London WC2. Founded as far eastern merchants in 1887, the company was in the pre-Second World War period one of the leading houses for Japanese general merchandise, including glass, china and fancy goods. Using their brand name "Fairylite", Graham Brothers were by 1953 advertising to the toy trade various novelties and toys ranging from "Mr. Potato Head" to "Double Tone Cow Horns." Similarly, L.D. Abraham Limited of Clerkenwell Green, London EC1, had been trading in Far Eastern textiles since 1890. Using the "Telsalda" name, Abraham was a major distributor of plastic toys in the 1960s and is still in existence today, although no longer involved in the toy trade.

Warren Cornelius, director of another London-based toy distributor, W.H.Cornelius Limited (founded in 1912), remembers the procedures followed in the early sixties when toy buyers from the British Isles started going in person to the Far East in search of suitable toy products. Contact with manufacturers in those days was made through agents. The factory representative—more often than not the owner himself—would meet with buyers around a table in the agent's office and show a range of his products. The manufacturer might be willing to make modifications to suit the buyers' wishes. In those days there was no need to worry about things like safety regulations, and any individual packaging would often be arranged separately by the importer/distributor rather than the manufacturer, which explains why many toys can be found with a different name on the box from the one on the product. A good deal of haggling would take place between manufacturer and buyer, but a price would eventually be agreed and an order placed.

In Britain, the toy import companies would show their wares at the various annual trade fairs—particularly the one held at Harrogate in Yorkshire—and would also employ a team of sales representatives who would go around to the wholesalers to show their line. In addition, Hong Kong manufacturers would come over to visit the trade fairs where they might pick up samples of metal toys, which they would take home and copy in plastic, usually to a larger scale. Many of these manufacturers were related through family connections and Hong Kong toys would themselves be copied by other companies.

Don Stephen and the Clifford Series

Another significant name in the toy distribution trade was Frederick Levy and Company of London. The founder was Jack Levy, who started trading in 1899, handing over to his younger brother Fred in 1922. Fred acquired premises in Tabernacle Street, London EC1 in the Finsbury Square area, where many other toy distributors and manufacturers such as Eisenmann, Cowan de Groot, L. D. Abraham, Mettoy, and Wells-Brimtoy had their offices. When Fred Levy died in 1942, his son Clifford took over as Chairman and Managing Director.

Mr. Don Stephen of F. Levy and Co., London, the first toy company to commission and distribute plastic Hong Kong friction cars in the United Kingdom under the name "Clifford Series."

The company was active in supplying toys to wholesalers and major stores throughout the British Isles. Levy and Company remained a family concern for many years but eventually ceased trading when it was sold to Herbert Kees in 1984 (a company which was still active in Hong Kong in the 1990s).

A key figure within F. Levy and Co. was Don Stephen, who was in charge of Sales and Purchasing from 1953 onwards, returning to the firm in the 1970s as a minority shareholder. Mr. Stephen has supplied a fascinating account of his involvement with Hong Kong toys in the early sixties, which answers many questions that collectors have often wondered about.

"Initially I took to Hong Kong with me samples of English-made cars such as Scalextric to demonstrate to the Hong Kong manufacturers what was required in finish and quality. We would commission a model such as an M.G. Sports or a Triumph TR 2 and give the factory a firm order, usually 12,000 dozen (sometimes less, sometimes more). They would then make the plastic tooling and mould. No one had made a metal friction motor in Hong Kong until I commissioned the first car. Only two factories at that time were willing and capable of having a friction motor made, Hong Kong Industrial Ltd (Mr. T.S. Loh) and Kader Industrial (Mr. L. Ting). The first models were made from Cellulose Acetate, a plastic that is banned from use today, but had an attractive sheen and a softish feel that was not brittle and was well-suited to making models. F. Levy never owned the moulds but had the right to exclusive sales coverage for the U.K., Eire, and some parts of Europe. All items were packaged in our own exclusive boxes and branded 'Clifford Series' [after company chairman Clifford Levy]."

The Clifford Series had the market to itself for almost two years, but soon other distributors jumped on the bandwagon; other Hong Kong factories themselves started making similar products, the best known being Lucky Toys. Among those known by the trademarks of British importers were Linda Toys, the "Emu" series, Laurie Toys, the "OK" brand, and Woolbro, denoting toys supplied exclusively to F. W. Woolworth Stores. Many similar Hong Kong toys were also distributed by the New Zealand-based Lincoln Industries, Louis Marx, and Cragstan of New York—companies which had earlier sourced their toys from Japan.

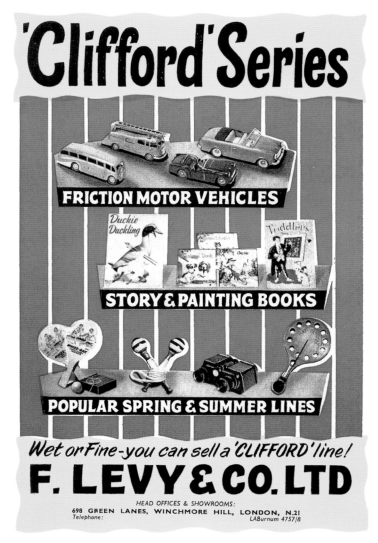

A 1961 Clifford Series trade advertisement. The bus and fire engine pictured are closely based on period Dinky Toys.

Winds of Change

As the years passed, Hong Kong toy companies developed in much the same way as their Japanese predecessors. Exactly the same criticisms that had earlier been made of Japanese toys were levelled at those from Hong Kong, and the response of the manufacturers was similar. The following comes from the October 1959 of the British toy trade journal *Toy and Game Manufacture*:

The [Hong Kong] manufacturers emphasise that there is no question of "dumping" Hong Kong toys in Britain, because nothing leaves the colony for this country except in response to a direct order from here.

Nevertheless, most of the key manufacturers now realise that the best way to enhance the reputation of their industry is by their own creative work, and more and more factories are now

employing artists and design staff to create their own products."[2]

By 1963 the Annual Report of the Federation of Hong Kong industries recorded "a significant advance in the quest for standards for Hong Kong products" and stressed that manufacturers were now aiming to conform with internationally recognised levels of quality.[3] A major aspect of this process was the question of safety. From time to time reports would appear in newspapers of cases such as the incident that occurred in July 1964, when four children from Bournemouth on the south coast of England were taken to hospital after sucking items from a toy tool kit which was found to have a high lead content.[4] The Hong Kong government responded quickly by setting up random tests for lead in plastic toys. Concerns were similarly expressed about celluloid dolls catching fire and the British Standards Institute issued a code of Safety Requirements for Children's Toys in November 1961 which recommended that celluloid should not be used in toys. British toy importers in turn required their suppliers to conform to these directives and by 1967 celluloid was no longer in general use for toy products.

On the business side, too, Hong Kong toy companies were rapidly changing, and larger ones such as Maks (at one time well-known for its water pistols), Jimson, NFIC, and Blue Box began to deal directly with distributors, bypassing the agents. A 1981 interview with a Hong Kong toy tycoon called Clayton Wong, published in *Toy Trader,* shows just how much things had changed. Among recent innovations, Wong mentions greater recognition of the importance of attractive package design; the ability of manufacturers to deal directly with clients by speaking English; the employment of trained personnel from outside Hong Kong as skilled product designers; and extended credit terms for clients. "Hong Kong is not cheap anymore," commented Wong, "but it's more reliable and the quality control is now so much better. Most manufacturers realise now that quality is important and if they don' t come up to scratch then they'll go out of business."[5]

But the final proof of the progress of Hong Kong's toy industry by the 1980s was that the main worry was now competition from Taiwanese toy makers, who were criticised for cheapness of quality and blatant copying of Hong Kong products—precisely the same charges made against Hong Kong twenty years before!

[1]*Games and Toys*, June 1959, p. 34
[2]*Toy and Game Manufacture*, October 1959, p. 6
[3]Quoted in *Games and Toys*, July 1963, p. 45
[4]Reported in *The Times*, July 17, 18, 24 1964
[5]*Toy Trader*, Volume 121, November 1981, p. 10

CHAPTER SIX

Plastic Friction Cars from Hong Kong

This chapter illustrates a selection of plastic friction-drive cars made in Hong Kong between the mid-1950s and the late 1960s. Tracking down the source of these can often be more difficult than in the case of Japanese tin toys as many are simply marked "Empire Made" or "Made in Hong Kong." Part of the explanation, as we saw in the previous chapter, is that these toys were often produced to meet the requirements of a particular toy distributor who would market them under his own trademark. But another reason for the reluctance of Hong Kong toymakers to put their names on their products may well be a desire to avoid accusations of unauthorized copying, for—as will immediately become evident from the photographs that follow—most of these were modelled on contemporary diecasts such as Dinky, Corgi, and Matchbox toys.

Yet it would be wrong to dismiss all Hong Kong toys as mere imitations. Even when the inspiration did come from a Dinky Toy the scale and colour would usually be altered and a friction drive motor would invariably be fitted. There are also plenty of toys which are original designs. A representative selection of both copies and originals will be found in the pages that follow and in most cases it has been possible to say something about either the maker or distributor. Obviously, the degree of realism varies considerably, but each item selected has something to commend it.

As far as the toy car enthusiast is concerned, the 1960s were the "golden years" for Hong Kong toys—even though few realised it at the time. But today these toys are around forty years old and exercise the same nostalgic appeal as their more highly-rated American, Japanese and European competitors. The pages that follow will give readers an idea of that appeal. How many more of these toys have yet to be discovered?

A 4.5-inch vintage Spyker distributed by Cragstan of New York. This is one of a number of models from Cragstan that are closely based on the Matchbox Yesteryear series. Yesteryear No. Y-16 was a Spyker in exactly the same colour scheme. *Courtesy of the Alex J. Cameron Collection.* $10.

Another Cragstan model, a 1941 Lincoln. This four-inch item has numerous fragile chrome fittings which are often missing. $20

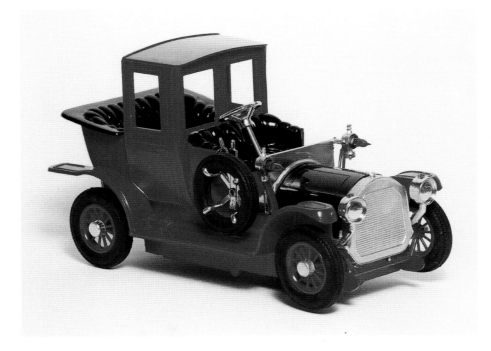

This nine-inch replica of a 1912 Packard is marked with the letters "NC" and the reference number 9002. It has a battery-operated motor and electric lights. Again, the model is based on a Matchbox Yesteryear, although it is to a considerably larger scale. *Courtesy of the Alex J. Cameron Collection.* $25–$35

An eight-inch replica of the 1959 Ford Thunderbird, with the Cragstan name on both model and box. Sold under reference number 1013-12, the model can be found in both convertible and hardtop versions and bears some resemblance to the smaller diecast by Corgi Toys. This is a sought-after item as it appeals to theme collectors who specialise in Fords in general, or Thunderbirds in particular. *Courtesy of the Alex J. Cameron Collection.* $45 each.

The makers of this six-inch Studebaker were careful to avoid giving any clues to its identity, describing it simply as a "Speedy Continental Sports Saloon." Several features of its design suggest that it is a fairly early example of the plastic friction car. For instance, the base is tin rather than plastic, and is stamped "Empire Made" rather than "Made in Hong Kong." Moreover, the colour is sprayed on as opposed to being moulded in the plastic, permitting a metallic paint to be used (both blue and bronze have been seen). A further unusual feature is that the interior details are made of cardboard. The model has some similarities to the version made by Dux of Germany. Again, this is an item particularly appreciated by Studebaker specialists. $35–45

Another early item marked "Empire Made," this six-inch Ford Convertible comes in both white with red seats or pink with blue seats—the texture and colour of the pink cellulose acetate being reminiscent of the material used to make plastic dolls in the fifties. The attractively illustrated box is marked "Emu Series," a trademark used by a London firm called S. Oppenheimer Ltd. and still to be found on novelty and stationery products to this day. Like many similar Hong Kong toys, the Ford is likely to be found in packaging with the names of other distributors too. Ford experts will note that the design of the front grille and lights reveals this model to be based on the 1956 prototype. $45

Comparable in size to the Ford, this is another interesting US car, based on a late 1940s Cadillac. The model is moulded in three sections: a base and interior in red, a lower body section in blue and a cream upper section. Marked Hong Kong 102 underneath, the only clue to its maker is the letters "JHT" on the rear license plate. Both the shape and the colour of the toy are remarkably similar to a diecast model by Renwal of the U.S.A. which is illustrated on page 419 of Paolo Rampini's *Golden Book of Model Cars*. *Courtesy of the Alex J. Cameron Collection.* $35+

Most plastic friction cars may have initially been commissioned by toy importers, but it was not long before some Hong Kong toy companies started to use their own trademarks. One of the largest of these was Lucky Toys who, predictably, used a horse-shoe emblem as their logo. The Studebaker Wagonaire—first modelled as a small scale diecast by Matchbox—was a good choice for a toy on account of the unusual sliding roof panel at the rear. At around 4.5 inches, this model, like other Lucky Toys, was smaller than many comparable Hong Kong friction toys. $15

The Morris Oxford was a typically British family saloon of the sixties, and yet the mainstream diecast makers ignored it, which makes this Hong Kong model all the more interesting. 9.5 inches in length, the Oxford has a compartment in the base to accommodate the batteries which power the car and the front and rear lights. There is no remote control box: the on/off switch is underneath, and the front wheels can be adjusted to make the car move to the left or right. Both the box and the car carry reference number 3356 and the brand name "OK." The distributor for this range in Britain was Don Bricks Ltd., of 530-4 Kingsland Road, London E8. Other OK products included a London Bus, a Morris Minor Telephones Van and a copy of the Dinky Supertoy Turntable Fire Escape, all of these having a particularly British flavour to them. $45–60

Another OK model of a Morris car, the 1100 saloon, which is powered in the same way as the Oxford. The steerable front wheels are of exactly the same design, but in this case an opening bonnet is fitted. Length 8 inches. *Courtesy of the Alex J. Cameron Collection.* $45

This MG 1100 is one of the many mystery items from Hong Kong: neither the model nor the box gives any clue to help identify the maker or distributor. The real car was made by BMC (the British Motor Company) whose "badge-engineering" policy led to Austin, Morris, MG, Wolseley and Riley versions being made. Like many Hong Kong products, the box artwork is the most appealing feature of this toy. $35

Another unidentified model of a British family car, the Austin 1800. Although the Austin was modelled by Dinky Toys and Spot-on, the Hong Kong version is not necessarily a direct copy. The styling of the real car may not be to everyone's taste, but the model is among the better quality plastic friction cars. Length 7.75 inches. *Courtesy of the Alex J. Cameron Collection.* $30

The Mini has always been a popular choice for diecast and plastic models. The blue car on the left is 6.5 inches long and carries the logo "TAT" underneath, plus a reference number (718). The estate car, which looks like a scaled-up version of a contemporary Dinky Toy, is 5.5 inches in length and is marked "NFIC." *Courtesy of the Alex J. Cameron Collection.* $30 each

This 7.5-inch Austin taxi is made of the harder, more brittle plastic used on earlier Hong Kong toys. Based on a long-running Dinky Toy model (which also came with a driver figure) the taxi is in a box marked "Fairylite," the trademark of Graham Bros., Far Eastern Merchants, of 73 Endell Street, London WC 2 but is marked with the name of the manufacturer—Mak's—underneath. The "taxi" sign on the roof is a paper sticker and there is also a sticker at the rear which states "Licensed to carry 4 persons." This is one of the harder to find Hong Kong models, made more desirable by its stylish box design. $60.

Vast numbers of plastic cars exist under the "Telsalda" label used by L.D. Abraham Ltd., based at Clerkenwell Green, London EC 1 in the early 1960s. The quality of these varies, no doubt because they were made by more than one manufacturer, whose name sometimes appears underneath the model. This Humber Sceptre carries the inscription "TAT 723 made in Hong Kong for Telsalda." It is fairly unusual to find both distributor's and maker's name. The Humber is a good quality, original design with plenty of operating features: opening luggage boot with spare wheel, roof rack and luggage, electrically-operated lights and even sliding side windows. $60

This Sunbeam Rapier coupe (5.5 inches) was made by Lucky Toys but distributed by Telsalda, and the toy is marked with both names. Later, many Lucky Toys were sold in boxes carrying that name, suggesting that this is one of the Hong Kong companies that became sufficiently well-established to distribute its own products directly. *Courtesy of the Alex J. Cameron Collection.* $30

Like Humber and Sunbeam, Hillman was part of the British Rootes Group which was eventually absorbed by Chrysler. The Hillman Imp was a small rear-engined car built at a new factory at Linwood in Scotland. Both the saloon and the stylish coupe carry the Telsalda name, but they are not necessarily made by the same manufacturer. *Courtesy of the Alex J. Cameron Collection.* $25 each.

This six-inch Imp is slightly smaller than the one by Telsalda and comes with an opening rear window (as on the real car), complete with two suitcases. The maker is Mak's, whose box illustrations are always very colourful. *Courtesy of the Alex J. Cameron Collection.* $35.

There are many different Hong Kong made Rolls Royces. This 7.5-inch Silver Cloud, distributed as part of the Clifford Series, is operated by a remote controller on the same principle as many of the Japanese tin cars. *Courtesy of the Alex J. Cameron Collection.* $40.

A good model of the Bentley Continental with an opening trunk containing a spare wheel and luggage. An advertisement in the British toy trade journal *Games and Toys* shows that the Bentley was also available with a caravan. Diecast collectors will recognise the similarity between the car and the Corgi version, while the caravan is clearly based on a Dinky original. *Courtesy of the Alex J. Cameron Collection.* $40

Trade advertisement from *Games and Toys*, November 1963, announcing the Bentley and caravan set.

This six-inch Rolls Royce is described as a Silver Cloud on the box but is more like the Silver Wraith modelled by Dinky Toys. Marked simply "Empire Made" underneath, it comes in a "Lincoln International" box. For background information on this New Zealand toy distributor, see the Glossary at the end of this book. $30

Another Rolls Royce, clearly marked on both box and model with the Lucky Toys name and horseshoe logo. This five-inch model, like several others pictured here, has an opening luggage compartment. $30

This Land Rover was inspired by a Corgi Toy model and carries the letters NFIC underneath. It comes with a removable canopy and is five inches in length. The box shows the British distributor to be Guitermann and Company. $35

Made of hard, brittle plastic, this Safari Land Rover is one of the earlier plastic friction toys to be distributed by its maker, Lucky Toys. It is unusual for a toy of this genre to be marked underneath with the words "registered design" followed by a serial number. The Land Rover is made in three sections: roof panel, main body, and chassis with seats moulded in. No window glazing is fitted. The box illustration is simple and stylised but very attractive. $60

These two Vauxhall Victor estate cars may take their inspiration from the Dinky Toy diecast, but again they are not direct copies. The red model, six inches in length, is by NFIC, while the larger (eight inch) one is marked CM. Both have an opening rear tailgate. NFIC, $25; CM, $35.

CM also made the Victor in saloon form. This version has a remote controller for the batteries with a simple forward/reverse movement without any steering mechanism. The luggage compartment opens to reveal two suitcases. The same car also came with a friction motor. $50

Although loosely based on Donald Campbell's 400 land speed record car "Bluebird," this model is orange rather than blue. The oversize wheels have clearly been borrowed from another product by the same unidentified maker. $15

This rather crude Jaguar D Type racing car is another early Lucky Toys product. $25

Linda Toys Jaguar 2.4 litre, similar to the Corgi diecast in style although slightly larger in size. Linda Toys were distributed in the UK by Randall and Wood Ltd., of Pentonville Road, London N1. $20–30

This nine-inch Jaguar 2.4 was distributed by Lincoln International and is marked "Empire Made." Most plastic toys were moulded in the appropriate body colour, but this item is unusual as it is painted. Several different versions have been noted: friction drive, battery-operated and freewheeling with a "steering column" inserted through the rear window opening, allowing the car to be pushed along and steered by means of a miniature steering wheel. $30–40

This trade advertisement from the May 1959 issue of *Games and Toys* shows another version of the Jaguar 2.4 in a smaller scale. *Courtesy of the British Library, London.*

May. 1959   GAMES & TOYS   81

Now! Lincoln International offer a range of new exclusive merchandise to major retailers!

Here's one typical example from our range of new toys at outstanding values made possible by cost saving minimum packs!

2.4 JAGUAR IN THE REPLICAR SERIES.

With these features:

★ Gleaming vacuumplated "chrome" detail
★ Opening boot with suitcase
★ 5¼" long
★ "Safety glass" windows throughout
★ Bright, sturdy plastic body on metal base
★ Smooth, long running Gyro motor
★ Attractively boxed
★ Retail price 2/11
★ Minimum pack 3 doz.

Write now for further details and an illustrated catalogue to

Lincoln International London Ltd.

59 St. Mary Axe, London, E.C.3.   Tel: AVE. 1888

This attractive combination of Jaguar Mark Ten and horse box trailer (complete with a plastic horse) again illustrates how Hong Kong toys can carry both maker's and distributor's names. The car and trailer are marked Lucky Toys whereas the box carries the trademark of the importer, Fairylite. With its fragile bumpers and separate door handles, the Jaguar would not have lasted long in the hands of a child. $30–40

Another Mark Ten Jaguar, this time by Mak's, whose boxes were amongst the most attractive of all Hong Kong toy companies. $25–30.

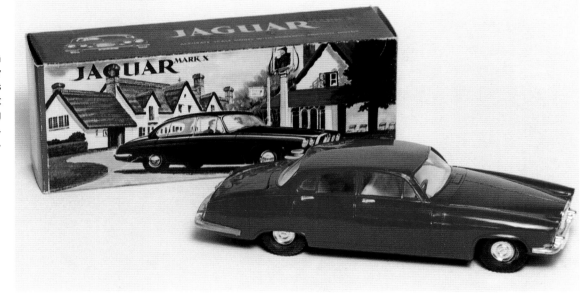

This E Type Jaguar was distributed by Marx and made in their own factory in Hong Kong. The hand controller allows for forward and reverse movements. $20–30

This Ford Zephyr is part of the "Replicar" series, distributed by Lincoln International. The top section of the body is moulded separately, allowing a convertible version to be created, as had frequently been done with Japanese tin toys. The hard, brittle plastic and the tinplate base identify this model as belonging to the earlier "Empire Made" era and it probably dates from c.1959-60. $20–30

The Ford Corsair was a British family car of the 1964–1970 era that fitted in between the Cortina and the larger Zephyr. This version, which has opening front doors, has no maker's name. The space on the box where there might have been a trademark has been blocked off, perhaps because the moulds for the toy passed from one owner to another. $20–30

Another, rather better finished, Corsair, marked with both the Lucky Toy and Telsalda names. As with the Humber Sceptre pictured earlier, there is an opening boot, roof rack and suitcase. Note the additional refinements such an a radio aerial and whitewall tires. *Courtesy of the Alex J. Cameron Collection.* $40

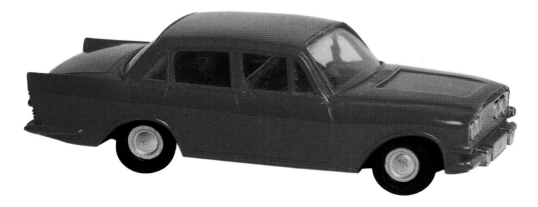

In the 1960s the Zodiac was Ford of Britain's top of the range model. This 6.5-inch replica was made by NFIC and distributed by Telsalda, both names being marked underneath. Strangely, no mainstream diecast of this imposing car was made at the time, although Airfix did offer a plastic construction kit from which the Hong Kong toy may have taken its inspiration. *Courtesy of the Alex J. Cameron Collection.* $30

A group of six cars distributed as a boxed set by the Clifford Series. (Left to right, top): Rover 90, Citroen DS19, Jaguar 2.4, all based on contemporary Corgi models. (Left to right, bottom): Sunbeam Rapier, Humber Hawk, Ford Consul Classic. *Courtesy of the Alex J. Cameron Collection.* $80 for the set.

At around four inches in length, each of these cars is more or less in scale with a Dinky Toy. The blue car (second from left) is a Rover 2000 with chrome plating and interior fittings. The others are of an earlier vintage and are typical of "cheap" Hong Kong products. The white car is a Standard Vanguard and the red one an Austin Cambridge. The blue and white car is a Vauxhall Cresta. It is possible that all four are loosely based on Corgi models. *Courtesy of the Alex J. Cameron Collection.* $10–15 each.

Dinky-size Vauxhall Victor (left) and Rover 2000 (right). These are better finished than many comparable toys. *Courtesy of the Alex J. Cameron Collection.* $10–15

Another, slightly larger, Rover and a Vauxhall Cresta with opening bonnet, both by Lucky Toys. These also come with chromed grilles, but the plating has been omitted on the two examples shown. *Courtesy of the Alex J. Cameron Collection.* $12–15

A seven-inch Citroen DS 19 with good quality box illustrations but no identification. $40

Two more Citroens: the yellow one in the foreground is from the Clifford Series and the black one is marked "TAT." Again, note the remarkably artistic box design. All three of these Citroens have some resemblance to the Corgi model. $25 each.

A six-inch Mercedes 300SL "Gullwing" coupe by Mak's, one of the better quality Hong Kong makes. $35

An accurate and quite elaborate ten-inch Mercedes 600 Pullman marked "Veny Toys" and distributed by Clifford. This has opening boot, bonnet and four doors and numerous fragile components such as half-open side windows and, of course, a three-pointed star mascot. $60

Two models of the Mercedes 220SE saloon. The blue car is six inches long and comes in a Clifford series box. The cream one is 8.5 inches long and is marked "OK." Both have an opening boot but the first model is friction powered whereas the OK model has an electric on/off switch underneath. $30 each.

Made of fairly cheap quality plastic, this remote control Mercedes 190SL carries no maker's name but has also been seen with the Louis Marx logo. This could mean that it was made by an unidentified manufacturer who at some stage supplied the model to Marx for distribution. $25–30

A six-inch friction-powered BMW 507 coupe by Mak's, reference number 2031. As there are relatively few models of this exotic vehicle, this one will have an obvious appeal to collectors who specialise in BMWs. $40

These three Volkswagens are marked with the letters "C.H." and the reference number 607. In addition to the colour variations, note that the blue car on the right has a different style of bumper and comes with a roof rack and row boat. On all three, the engine compartment opens. *Courtesy of the Alex J. Cameron Collection.* $30 each.

This Volkswagen is another model from the Linda Toys series, also marked "Tat" on both the car and the box flap. $30

Many Hong Kong toys are marked simply with the initials of the maker. This six-inch VW 1500, with opening front luggage compartment, is based on a Dinky Toy original and carries the letters "H.P." It has been seen in red or blue. The 5.5-inch caravan is copied from a plastic model made by Politoys of Italy. Hong Kong toymakers were often quite happy to borrow ideas from more than one source to create something new. *Courtesy of the Alex J. Cameron Collection.* $40 (for the set).

Models of Volkswagen Vans are almost as popular as the Beetle itself. The six-inch Microbus on the left is no. 605 in the C.H. range and is fitted with an opening rear door. The yellow Camper Van is five inches long and was made for Telsalda by Jimson. *Courtesy of the Alex J. Cameron Collection.* $35 each.

A very simple but appealing model of a Bubble Car, carrying no maker's name. The plastic Shell petrol pumps are very much in 1960s style but were still on sale in the 1980s. *Courtesy of the Alex J. Cameron Collection.* Bubble car, $30; Petrol pumps, $12.

Another example of a Hong Kong model being influenced by another product without being a direct copy. The rear of this van is similar to the "Pickford's" Removals Van in the Matchbox series, but it comes with advertising for a number of well-known British food brands such as Cadbury's Chocolate and John West Salmon. *Courtesy of the Alex J. Cameron Collection.* $20 each

Another unidentified maker copied the Dinky Toy Euclid tipper truck, even fitting a similar type of tipping mechanism, although the toy was not nearly as robust as the Dinky original which still turns up frequently today. $15

This attractive fuel tanker is something of a hybrid. The cab (based on an A.E.C. proto-type) is similar to a Dinky model, whereas the trailer is based on a Corgi design. The maker is Lucky Toys, who also issued an articulated covered truck with the same cab unit. $40

This impressive fifteen-inch car transporter is clearly based on a very similar model made by Norev of France. Many Hong Kong plastic toys are scaled-up versions of diecasts, whereas the Norev original not only has similar dimensions but is also made of plastic. The two car designs are a Simca and a Citroen. *Courtesy of the Alex J. Cameron Collection.* $60

This fire engine with extending ladders was distributed as part of the Clifford Series but is marked underneath with the maker's name, Jimson. The inspiration clearly came from the Matchbox Merryweather Fire Escape. The "siren," noted on the box as a special feature, is nothing more than the noise made by the friction motor! $20–30

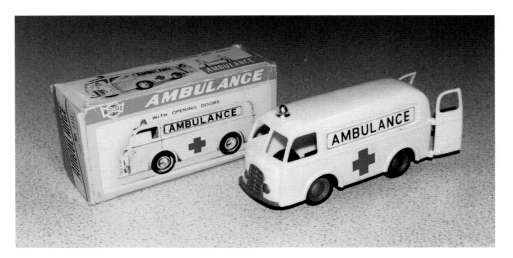

"Woolbro" was a trademark used by F.W. Woolworth stores. This Ambulance, with a Karrier cab style and opening rear doors, is a very simple toy indeed, but it does have the merit of being an original design. $20

Unlike the Ambulance on the previous page, this Ford Transit Police Van by Telsalda is an exact copy of a contemporary Dinky Toy. Even the license plate—INJ 72 E—is the same. $30

This Commer TV Service van, marked "Mertrade" (presumably a distributor) is a scaled-up version of a small Match-box model which also had a ladder, TV sets and aerials on the roof. $30

No vehicle was modelled more frequently in Hong Kong than the London double-decker bus. The reason was that these toys were often sold as souvenirs in shops and street stalls. Model London buses are still sold through these channels today, although they are now sourced from China rather than Hong Kong. The rear-entrance Routemaster is the most popular choice but the model shown here represents the Leyland Atlantean and was sold under the Telsalda name. The wheels are clearly more suited to a sports car than a bus! $20

Two single-deck buses. The blue one by Mak's (left) resembles the Matchbox Bedford Duple Coach and the other (by an unknown maker) echoes the appearance of the Dinky Supertoy Wayne School Bus. $30 each.

In 1963 Dinky Toys made a diecast model of the Vega Major Luxury Coach and several copies of this were made in Hong Kong. This one, by N.F.I.C., is twelve inches long. *Courtesy of the Alex J. Cameron Collection.* $30.

Another, smaller, Vega Major, marked simply "V" underneath. The "Salco" name on the box refers to a British distributor, A. Saalheimer and Co. As on the Dinky model, the front axles steer and the boot opens. $20

Described simply as a "Travelling Car," this coach is based on a Mercedes. The idea of making the top half in transparent material was probably borrowed from German manufacturers such as Hammer and Schuco whose buses use this technique. $25

A delightful little set of racing cars, each one less than two inches long. From left to right, the cars represent a Connaught, Mercedes-Benz, Ferrari, Vanwall, and Maserati, all of which had been made by Dinky Toys. The box reads "A Garage Full of Automobiles" and "Elm Toys—Empire Made." *Courtesy of the Alex J. Cameron Collection.* $30

Blue Box was a prolific manufacturer of plastic toy cars is various sizes, with a particular fondness for those in Matchbox scale. Many early Matchbox models were copied and sold either individually or in sets of four. The pale green Ford Thames (left) is for some reason described as a "furniture van." The boxed set consists of a London bus, Commer van, Bedford Tipper and Morris pickup. Individual models, $8; set, $30.

The four items in the Civil Engineering set are again closely copied from Matchbox models. As well as being collectible in their own right, these models also appeal to some Matchbox collectors. $30

"Auto Series," another Blue Box set, containing (left to right) a Hillman Minx, Jaguar XK120, Ford Station Wagon, and M.G.A. sports. Once again, these are almost exact copies of Matchbox originals. $30

This time Blue Box turned to a French manufacturer for inspiration: Norev. This Unic car transporter appeared in the Norev 1/86 Micro-Miniatures series, although it did not come with the same cars. *Courtesy of the Alex J. Cameron Collection.* $20

Another group of Matchbox copies. Close examination of these shows that they are not in fact the same as those in the Blue Box series, showing that it often happened that similar toys would be made by different Hong Kong manufacturers, who sometimes even copied each other! The name on the header card, Alden International, refers to the U.S. distributor. *Courtesy of the Alex J. Cameron Collection.* $20

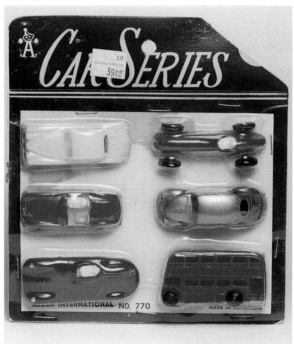

Another selection of unidentified Hong Kong cars in a smaller scale, once again derived from Matchbox products, although the horse box pulled by the tractor is more like a model in the Dinky Dublo series. *Courtesy of the Alex J. Cameron Collection.* $6–8 each.

Although plastic was the usual material for Hong Kong toys in the 1960s, some diecasts were made. This Mercedes Benz is one of a group of seven- or eight-inch cars variously distributed by Lincoln International, Cragstan, and—for the Japanese market—Yonezawa. The box lists others in the series. Like most Hong Kong cars, these are friction powered. $30–40

Another of the Lincoln/ Cragstan larger diecasts, a fairly accurate US export VW Beetle, sought after by specialist Volkswagen collectors and therefore the most desirable of this series. *Courtesy of the Alex J. Cameron Collection.* $70+

This Volkswagen by Playart is a suitable item with which to end this survey of Hong Kong products. Dating from the early 1970s, it marks the transition from plastic friction cars to diecasts in approximately 1/43 scale. It may not be quite as good as contemporary European products, but it was not long before the established manufacturers were sub-contracting to Hong Kong—the beginning of a process which has today led to almost all the world's diecast toy manufacture taking place in the Far East. *Courtesy of the Alex J. Cameron Collection.* $20

Checklist of Early Japanese Diecasts

Model Pet Series
1959 Onwards

1	Toyota Crown
2	Toyota Masterline Estate Car
2SA	Toyota Masterline Ambulance
3	Subaru 360
4	Toyota Land Cruiser
5	Datsun Bluebird
6	Prince Skyline
7	Toyota Corona
8	Austin Cambridge
9	Hillman Minx
10	Nissan Cedric
10ST	Nissan Cedric Taxi
11	Toyota Corona Estate Car
12	Toyota Crown
12SP	Toyota Crown Police Car
13	Mazda 360
14	Toyota Publica
15	Prince Skyline Convertible
16	Prince Skyline Coupe
17	Datsun Bluebird
18	Isuzu Bellet
19	Toyota Sports Coupe
20	Toyota Crown (1963 and 1964 versions)
20SP	Toyota Crown Police Car
21	Toyota Masterline Estate Car
21SA	Toyota Masterline Ambulance
22	Prince Gloria
22T	Prince Gloria Taxi
23	Toyota Land Cruiser (with canopy)
24	Mitsubishi Colt
25	Datsun Bluebird 1965
26	Hino Contessa 1300
27	Toyota Corona (1965 and 1966 versions)
29	Hino Contessa Coupe
30	Mazda Familia
31	Toyota Sports 800
32	Nissan Silvia Coupe

33	Nissan Cedric
34	Honda S800 Sports
35	Honda S800 Coupe
36	Toyota 2000GT
37	Honda N360
38	Toyota Crown Super
39	Toyota Crown Coupe
40	Mitsubishi Galant
41	Toyota Crown Police Car
43	Honda RC 162 Motorcycle
44	Suzuki 750 GT Motorcycle
45	Nissan Skyline 2000GT
46	Yamaha XS 650-E Motorcycle
47	Datsun Sunny Coupe 1400
48	Honda CB750 Motorcycle
50	Honda CB750 Police Motorcycle
51	Toyota Corona Mk I 2000GSS
52	Datsun Bluebird UHT
54	Nissan Cedric 2600GX
55	Toyota Crown Taxi
56	Toyota Crown Fire Car
57	Toyota Crown Ambulance
58	Mitsubishi Galant Rally Car
59	Nissan Skyline Rally Car
60	Yamaha Police Motorcycle/Sidecar
61	Yamaha Police Motorcycle
62	Yamaha Motorcycle/Sidecar
101	Toyota Toyoace Truck
102	Toyota Toyoace Truck/Canopy
103	Honda Motorcycle

Micro Pet Series
1961 Onwards

1	Subaru 360
2	Datsun Bluebird
5	Nissan Cedric
6	Prince Skyline Estate Car
7	Mazda 360

8 Toyota Corona
9 Chevrolet Impala
10 Chevrolet Impala Police Car
11 Prince Skyway Estate Car
12 Ford Falcon
13 Ford Falcon Police Car
14 Prince Microbus
15 Hillman Minx
17 Datsun Bluebird Estate Car
18 Nissan Light Truck
19 Isuzu Bellet 2000

Notes
1. Numbers 2, 5, 6, 7, 8, 9, 14 and 17 were also produced in a chrome-plated finish.
2. There are two separate versions of the Datsun Bluebird no. 2, representing different model years.
3. Two different grille designs can be found on the Hillman Minx no. 15.

Miniature Pet Series
1962

1 Opel Kapitan

Cherryca Phenix Series
1962 Onwards

1 Hino Contessa
2 Nissan Cedric Station Wagon
3 Mercedes Benz 300SL Roadster
4 1932 Datsun (chrome finish)
5 Chevrolet Impala
6 Buick Electra
7 Ford Falcon
8 Volkswagen 1200
9 Volkswagen Karmann Ghia Roadster
10 Dodge Polara
11 Mercedes Benz 300SL Hardtop
12 Datsun 1200 Station Wagon
13 Datsun 1200 Pickup
14 Isuzu Bellel De Luxe
15 Ford Thunderbird
16 Datsun Fairlady Roadster
17 Lincoln Continental
18 Mercedes Benz 220SE

19 Citroen DS 19 Convertible
20 Cadillac 62 Special
21 1912 Chevrolet (chrome finish)
22 Datsun Bluebird
23 Jaguar E Type Roadster
24 Prince Gloria
25 Nissan Cedric
26 Toyota Crown
27 Toyota Crown Station Wagon
28 Toyota Corona
29 Mercedes Benz 300SL Roadster
30 Isuzu Bellet
31 Prince Skyline 1500
32 Datsun Bluebird
33 Mitsubishi Colt
34 Hino Contessa
35 Nissan Cedric Taxi
36 Toyota Crown Police Car
37 Toyota Crown Taxi
38 Honda S 600 Roadster
39 Prince Sport Coupe
40 Toyota Corona Coupe
41 Daihatsu Compagno
42 Mitsubishi Debonair
43 Nissan Cedric Police Car
44 Mazda Luce
45 Mitsubishi Colt
46 Datsun Bluebird Rally
47 Nissan Skyline Rally
48 Prince Gloria Rally
50 Isuzu Bellet GT

FL-1 Buick Electra
FL-2 Ford Falcon

Marusan
Date Unknown

8501 Panhard Articulated Truck
8502 Morris Royal Mail Van
8503 Daimler Ambulance
8504 Ford Milk Truck
8505 Observation Coach
8506 Euclid Dump Truck
8507 Austin "Service Car"
Toyota Toyoace Truck

Sources: Works by Kelly, Rampini and Sasamoto. (See bibliography for details).

Glossary of Manufacturers and Trademarks

In 1964 there were an estimated 2,000 toy manufacturers in Japan, with an annual production of almost $150 million. The number of factories in Hong Kong producing plastic toys rose from 300 in 1959 to 1,200 in 1965. Inevitably, then, only a tiny proportion of these toy makers can be identified. Most, no doubt, would be very small operations working as sub-contractors for much larger concerns and their products would carry the name of the distributor, with the result that the actual makers of many of these toys will never be known. What follows is some background information on just a few of the biggest names.

Asahi Trading Company (ATC): Founded in 1955, Asahi was both an importer and exporter of toys based in Taito Ku, Tokyo. The company pioneered the importation of European and American toys to Japan in the sixties, such as Lone Star, Mettoy, Monogram, AMT, Dinky, and Corgi. Its own products included electric and friction cars in addition to educational toys. Asahi's sixteen-inch Chrysler Imperial is generally considered to represent the highest level of realism ever attained in tinplate. In 1964 Asahi was reported in the toy trade as being present at the Nurnberg toy fair, representing nine Japanese toy firms. Asahi started making the Model Pet series of diecasts in 1959, with the last new addition to the range appearing in 1973. By 1979 the company was bankrupt and is today under the ownership of Casio Computers. The name Asahi means "rising sun."

Alps Shoji Co. Ltd: Founded in 1948, Alps originally specialised in cloth toy animals with clockwork mechanisms but became best known for their toy vehicles. Alps' finest tin toys were the 1956 Chrysler New Yorker and the 1953 Packard.

Bandai: Bandai offered a larger selection of tin cars than any other Japanese firm, particularly the "Automobiles of the World Series," which extended to over 100 items and was notable for including numerous European and Japanese subjects in addition to more usual American ones. A characteristic of Bandai tin toys is the black baseplate with intricate chassis detailing in silver-gray. These toys can also be recognised by their trademark, a stylised capital "B." Bandai was founded by Naoharu Yamashina who, finding that business was slow in textiles, started to sell toys in 1947 and began making his own in 1950. Bandai was still producing tin cars in the 1970s, although production had by then been moved to Korea. Today, Bandai is the third largest toy company in the world, with 53 subsidiaries in eighteen countries. Bandai manufactured the first generation of electronic games and had huge success in the 1990s with new lines like Power Rangers and the Tamagotchi. The founder, Mr Yamashina, died in October 1997.

Blue Box: A Hong Kong firm which made many different plastic toys, often based on other products, particularly a large series of copies of Matchbox toys. Blue Box was still a significant company in the 1980s, with offices in Kowloon, New York, Milan and Manchester, England.

Cragstan: the name of this New York toy importer and distributor is believed to be a contraction of that of the founder, Craig Stanton. Cragstan would place bulk orders with Far Eastern toy companies, and would be in a position to specify exactly what kind of product it wanted. Thus, many Cragstan products carry both the distributor's and the manufacturer's name on the box. Cragstan's inventory was huge, including not only cars but tinplate aircraft, robots, astronauts, railway locomotives and novelty figures. What these all had in common was the ingenuity of their mechanisms. Their "Shaking Car," for instance, was a vintage car that would move back or forward, stop and shake from side to side. This product was made by TN. Later, Cragstan also distributed diecast and plastic cars made in Hong Kong.

Haji: Founded in 1951, Haji was a Japanese manufacturer of tin toy cars and mechanical figures.

Their masterpiece was undoubtedly the 1956 Ford convertible.

Ichiko Kogyo: Japanese manufacturer of tin toy cars. Ichiko was described in a report on the Third Japan International Toy Fair of 1964 as "the main producer of friction cars," some of the largest being up to 33 inches long. As with most brands, quality was inconsistent, their best piece probably being the 1959 Buick. Police cars were an Ichiko favourite, and the company had close links with ATC.

Kosuge Toys: Early Japanese brand name, maker of one of the first post-war military Jeep toys.

Kuramochi Shoten: A leading pre-war Japanese toy brand which made a small group of diecasts for the American market after the war under the name "Collectoys." These were distributed by Linemar.

Kokyu Shokai: Identified by Kitahara in *Cars: Tin Toy Dreams* as the maker of the tinplate Austin Cambridge (see page 65). Some excellent Volvos and an Opel exist marked KS, but are not necessarily made by the same firm.

Lincoln: Lincoln Industries grew out of a New Zealand retail business called Farmers Trading Company. The Managing Director was Mr. A. Lincoln Laidlaw, described in a 1965 toy trade journal as a "Globe Trotting Tycoon" on account of the fact that by this period Lincoln had offices in Hong Kong and London as well as New Zealand. Like Cragstan, Lincoln Industries distributed a large amount of Hong Kong-sourced products such as plastic friction and electric cars. In 1957 they were advertising plastic construction kits and in 1963 their lines included battery-operated hair dryers and food mixers, a slot race set, and a Junior Engineer Construction Set (like Meccano). The company seems to have been good at promoting these products, too, running competitions in children's comics, issuing a quarterly newsletter *(Lincoln News)* to the UK toy trade and advertising on British television.

Linemar: Linemar was a Japanese subsidiary of the American Marx toy empire. The name appears on numerous tin cars, Disney, and other novelty items. Aware that the American toy industry could not withstand Japanese competition, Louis Marx later became the first American toy manufacturer to start a toy factory in Hong Kong (in 1956).

Marusan Shoten: Although Marusan made many tin cars, the name is associated with a trio of superior items: the 1950-51 Cadillac, 1956 Chevrolet, and 1956 Ford. Marusan also made dolls, a small group of diecasts based on British and French Dinky Toys, and was the pioneer of Japanese plastic aircraft construction kits. The Marusan name was later found on a remote-control fantasy dragon, Godzilla, reissued in the seventies under the Bullmark name. Incidentally, the word "Shoten," often found after toy company names, simply means "store" or "shop."

Masudaya: Masudaya's origins go back as far as 1724 and the name is still going strong today. With a turnover of 30 million US dollars in 1997-98, the Masudaya Corporation's current business field covers toys, games, interior goods, and computer games. Among their tin toy vehicles were a clockwork De Soto made in the 1930s and an early "oval window" Volkswagen. Masudaya pioneered a wireless remote-control robot in around 1958 and used the same technology to produce early radio-controlled vehicles like the fourteen-inch-long "Radicon" single deck bus and the Oldsmobile shown on page 35. The letter T on top of an M inside a diamond-shaped logo (standing for Modern Toys) is identified in Dale Kelley's book as a trademark used by Masudaya.

Nomura: Toys with the trademark "TN" were made by Nomura, a company whose origins date back to 1923. According to the 1964 Toy Fair report, Nomura pioneered electric toys in Japan and at that time claimed to be "the largest producer of metal toys in the country. Since the inception of T.V. in Japan, the company has extended its production to include a variety of T.V. characters."

SSS: This company produced a fine Cadillac, and marketed many tin trucks. They also marketed some smaller tin friction cars in boxed sets under the name "Tiny Giant Senior Series," one of these being a group of six assorted European cars (Mercedes, Rolls Royce, Ferrari, Citroen, Opel, MG). This is one of a number of companies known only by its initials; there is also SS, which appears to be a separate firm altogether. According to Kitahara's book *Tin Toy Dreams*, SS stands for Shibuya Seisakusyo.

Yonezawa: Another of the major tinplate companies, many of their cars being of high quality. The company takes it name from the founder, Mr. Yoshitaka Yonezawa. From a detailed run of Yonezawa trade catalogues it has been possible to form an overview of the total inventory of this firm which in the early sixties used the trade name "Cherry Y Brand." Most Yonezawa products carry the logo of a letter Y inside a "leaf" pattern. Tinplate cars were a major product line, but by no means

国産車を網羅する
ダイヤペット1/40
シリーズ。
集める楽しさ…
その一台一台に
ヨネザワの
最新技術が生かさ
れています。

MINI-CAR SERIES

ミニカー
シリーズ

品番	品　　　名	全国売価
D－162	トヨタ2000GT	550円
D－163	ニッサンR380	450円
D－164	ニッサングロリア	400円
D－165	ワーゲン1300	400円
D－166	マツダコスモ	550円
D－167	ベンツ230S	400円
D－168	ホンダN360	500円
D－169	ホンダS800	500円
D－170	ニュークラウン	
D－171	ニューブルーバード	550円
D－172	スズキフロンテ	
D－173	マツダファミリアロータリークーペ	580円

the only one. Numerous railway engines, single deck buses, tanks, aircraft, trucks, and fire engines were made too but these are far less realistic and many are non-prototypical. The emphasis was on play value rather than accuracy, hence the fondness for fire engines with extending ladders, convertible cars with retractable roofs, and battery-operated robots with "stop and go" action. Yonezawa also made plush-covered mechanical dogs and other animals, toy guns, telephones, space rockets, electric slot car sets, and model railways. 1965 was a significant year as diecast toy cars were in-

troduced under the Diapet name. Later catalogues reveal that Yonezawa also imported foreign diecasts and sold these alongside its own products, such as the Sabra range of American cars made in Israel and the Sablon series of European cars from Belgium. Today, Yonezawa is part of Sega Enterprises Limited, and Sega Yonezawa is still listed as a subsidiary company.

A page from a catalogue issued in the late 1950s by Cragstan, showing a variety of tinplate toys. The 9.25-inch Ford Convertible with retractable top is typical of the best of Cragstan lines, having an ingenious mechanism which allowed the roof to retract automatically into the trunk area. Like other companies, Cragstan was quite happy to offer a mixture of large and fairly realistic tin toys alongside simpler items. *Courtesy of Douglas R. Kelly*

Opposite page:
A page from the 1969 Yonezawa catalogue, showing some of the Diapet series of diecasts. The Mercedes convertible in the middle of the second row from the front appears to be the model originally issued under the Cherryca Phenix name. Some of the others, however, are American cars manufactured by Gamda Koor of Israel, showing that Yonezawa distributed other companies' products as well as making its own.

#10433—LEVER ACTION POLICE & FIRE DEPT. CARS —ASSORTED
Pull the lever on this 8¼" long 1959 Police car and Fire Dept. patrol car and watch these cars go! Individually boxed and packed assorted.
Ctn. Pk. 4 doz.—8 lbs. per doz.

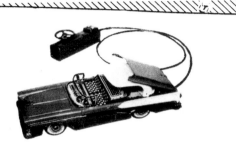

#40101—B.O./R.C. FORD "STEEL TOP" CONVERTIBLE
9¼" long remote control, battery operated Ford Skyliner "steel top" convertible that goes forward and reverse and is steered automatically left and right. While in motion, the steel convertible top can go into the trunk area, automatically simulating the actual Ford "steel top" convertible. Individually boxed — 2 "D" batteries.
Ctn. Pk. 1 doz.—23 lbs. per doz.

#10634—"PRESS-PUSH" PISTON RACER
Just press down on this 9½" streamlined racer and when you let go watch the pistons move as the car races. Individually boxed.
Ctn. Pk. 6 doz.—7 lbs. per doz.

#10635—FRICTION STATION WAGON WITH BOAT & CARRIER
11½" long, authentically detailed 3 piece combination, consisting of a friction station wagon, a boat carrier and an all metal boat that floats. Individually boxed.
Ctn. Pk. 6 doz.—6 lbs. per doz.

#10636—FRICTION SEDAN & HOUSE TRAILER
The latest in house trailer design is included in this 11" long toy. The sedan has a friction motor and the trailer has an action door and an awning which opens and closes over the rear window. Individually boxed.
Ctn. Pk. 6 doz.—8 lbs. per doz.

#10437—FRICTION M G CONVERTIBLE
9½" long England's finest sports car. Individually boxed.
Ctn. Pk. 4 doz.—8 lbs. per doz.

#10438—FRICTION PROP-ROD PISTON ACTION RACER
This prop-rod racer has spinning prop in rear which activates six brightly colored pistons. Everything is moving and when this 9" prop-rod racer gets going—clear the roads! Individually boxed.
Ctn. Pk. 4 doz.—11 lbs. per doz.

#10639— FRICTION TRACTOR
A 7" long friction Tractor—the latest model with four heavy duty rubber tractor tires. Individually boxed.
Ctn. Pk. 6 doz.—6 lbs. per doz.

136 FIFTH AVENUE, N.Y. • OR 5-8000

BIBLIOGRAPHY

The following works have been consulted in the course of the writing of this book, and are recommended for further reading:

Allen, G. C. *A Short Economic History of Modern Japan* (4th Edition, Macmillan Press, London, 1981)

Bath, Leslie Hurle. *A Potted History of the Japanese Miniature Car* (article published in *Modellers' World Magazine*, Vol. 8, No. 3, April 1979, pp. 8 -9)

Box, Rob de la Rive. *Encyclopaedia of Classic Cars* (Rebo Productions Ltd, the Netherlands, 1999)

Flammang, James M., et al., *Ford Chronicle: A Pictorial History from 1893* (Publications International, Ltd., Lincolnwood, Illinois, 1997)

Gibson-Downs, Sally and Gentry, Christine. *Motorcycle Toys: Antique and Contemporary* (Collector Books, Paducah, Kentucky, 1995)

Gurski, Jeffrey C. *Greenberg's Guide to Cadillac Models and Toys* (Greenberg Publishing Co., Sykesville, Maryland, 1992)

Hermans, Marc and Sabatès, Fabien. *Encyclopédie des Jouets et Miniatures Citroen* (Retroviseur, Paris, 1995)

Ho, Yin-Ping. *Trade, Industrial Restructuring and Development in Hong Kong* (Macmillan, London, 1992)

Kelley, Dale. *Collecting the Tin Toy Car, 1950–1970* (New Cavendish Books, London, 1985)

Kelly, Douglas R. *Die Cast Price Guide* (Antique Trader Books, Dubuque, Iowa, 1997)

Kellman, Jerold L., et al. *Cars of the 50s* (Consumer Guide Magazine Classic Car Quarterly, Volume 205, Fall 1978)

Kitahara, Teruhisa. *Cars: Tin Toy Dreams* (Chronicle Books, San Francisco, 1985)

Kitahara, Teruhisa and Shimizu, Yukio. *1000 Tin Toys* (Taschen, Cologne, 1996)

Nakajima, Noboru. *Model Cars of the World* (Hoikusha Publishing, Osaka, Japan, 1977)

Nakamura, Takafusa. *The Postwar Japanese Economy* (University of Tokyo Press, Tokyo, 1981)

Rampini, Paolo. *The Golden Book of Model Cars, 1900–1975* (Edizioni Paolo Rampini, Milan, 1995)

Sasamoto, Kenji, et al. *All About Japanese Miniature Cars* (Neko Publishing Ltd, Japan, 1996)

Siuru, Bill. *Illustrated Micro and Mini Car Buyer's Guide* (Motorbooks International, Osceola, WI, 1995)

Sordet, Michel. *Ma Collection No. 21*, September 1979

Sterling, Bruce. *The Best Fifties Fords* (article published in *Antique Toy World Magazine*, October 1989, pp. 24–27.)

Walter, Gerhard G. *Tin Dream Machines: German Tinplate Toy Cars and Motorcycles of the 1950s and 1960s* (New Cavendish Books, London, 1996)